LEE ALLAN SMITH: OKLAHOMA'S BEST FRIEND

Publication made possible by:

LOUISE & CLAYTON I. BENNETT

CHRISTY & JIM EVEREST

RAY ACKERMAN

BANK OF OKLAHOMA, N.A.

LIBBY & G. T. BLANKENSHIP

BOB BURKE

JACKIE COOPER

NANCY & ED DE CORDOVA

CARLA & RICHARD ELLIS

JOSEPHINE W. FREEDE

KERR-MCGEE CORPORATION

ANGUS & JODI MCQUEEN

HERMAN MEINDERS

BARRY SWITZER

J. BLAKE WADE

Television Mobile Unit WKY
THE OKLAHOMAN AND TIMES STATION
OKLAHOMA CITY

LEE ALLAN SMITH: OKLAHOMA'S BEST FRIEND

by **Bob Burke** *and*
Gini Moore Campbell

foreword by **David L. Boren**

edited by Eric Dabney

OKLAHOMA
HERITAGE
ASSOCIATION

Oklahoma City

Contents

Acknowledgments

It *was a difficult task* to convince Lee Allan Smith to allow his biography to be published. We began asking nearly a decade ago. Each time the subject arose, he directed us to other people. First, to Abe Lemons, then to Ray Ackerman and others. Lee Allan's consistent comment was, "You should write about them. They have done great things for Oklahoma. I'm only working with them."

Those close to Lee Allan know that he does not promote Oklahoma for personal credit or attention. There is no doubt he genuinely loves his native state and has worked tirelessly for more than a half century to make it a better place to live. When he is promoting another grandiose event, he thinks big. His eyes sparkle when he thinks of a new wrinkle to gain Oklahoma excellence when he says, "Wouldn't it be wonderful to.........?" His mind is always working. Oklahoma has benefited greatly from his wisdom, charm, and extraordinary gift for planning and completing hundreds of events.

Much of the information about Lee Allan's life was obtained from his family, friends, and associates. Thanks to the following people who granted interviews: Ray Ackerman, Bob Barry, Clay Bennett, Coca Bell, Jimmy Webb, G.T. Blankenship, David Boren, Elizabeth Brunsdon, Dick Burpee, Joe Castiglione, Jack Catlett,

5

Sharyn Chesser, B.C. Clark, Jr., Dick Clements, Luke Corbett, Larry Nichols, Josephine Freede, Jim Couch, Eddie Crowder, Ed de Cordova, Dick Ellis, Mick Evenson, Randy Everest, Curt Gowdy, Burns Hargis, Carolyn Hill, Kirk Humphreys, Jane Jayroe, Ronnie Kaye, Jennifer Kiersch, Ed Martin, Tom McDaniel, Buck McPhail, Angus McQueen, Herman Meinders, Bobby Murcer, Pam Newby, Steve Owens, Gene Rainbolt, Dee Sadler, Chuck Schroeder, George Short, Ann Smith, Linda Brown, Larry Payton, and Carroll Swickey.

Interviews also were granted by Dean Smith, DeAnn Smith, DeLee Smith, Sugar Smith, Wendy Smith, John Snodgrass, Gary Story, Paul Strasbaugh, Tom Sturdivant, Bill Thrash, Joe Dan Trigg, Martha Pat Upp, Blake Wade, Joe Washington, Kari Watkins, Danny Williams, Silkey Wilson, Bill Winkler, Fred Zahn, Susie Vessels, Ann Alspaugh, Ctaci Combs, Jackie Cooper, Sandy Garrett, Marion DeVore, Tom Dulaney, Jim Greenwald, Frank Keating, Cathy Kirk, Dave Maloney, Bob Naifeh, George Nigh, Jim Norick, Darrell Royal, Lee Stidham, Bob Stoops, Mike Turpen, Sandy Unitas, Sidney and Marylin Upsher, Jane Harlow, Dave Lopez, Ron Norick, Bill Robinson, Nadie Smith, Leland Gourley, Ed Joullian III, Tim O'Toole, Barry Switzer, Bob Hoover, and Vince Gill.

Thanks to Linda Lynn, Mary Phillips, Melissa Hayer, Robin Davison, and Billie Harry at the archives of the Oklahoma Publishing Company. We sincerely appreciate the encouragement of Clay Bennett and the efforts of our editor, Eric Dabney, and our proof-readers, George and Marcia Davis. We are deeply indebted to the Oklahoma Heritage Association, through its chairman, Roxana Lorton, and president, Shannon L. Nance, for its continuing com-mitment to preserve Oklahoma's incredible historic journey.

—BOB BURKE
—GINI MOORE CAMPBELL
2005

by david l. boren

I am a huge fan of Lee Allan Smith. His many contributions to Oklahoma, and in particular the University of Oklahoma, are significant.

He has been a great supporter of OU, raising money for everything from uniforms for the Pride of Oklahoma marching band to assisting us with Edward L. Gaylord in funding the Journalism School and Memorial Stadium projects.

Lee Allan has helped coordinate many alumni events. I will never forget his suggestion that OU hire former Big Eight Commissioner Chuck Neinas as an advisor in our search for an athletic director and head football coach. Fortunately, I took his advice and the Sooners ended up with Joe Castiglione and Bob Stoops, who quickly put us on the road to rebuilding OU Athletics.

Lee Allan and University of Oklahoma President David L. Boren, right.

7

Lee Allan has been a major factor in the success of many programs that benefit Oklahomans. His leadership can be seen in the nationally-televised *Stars and Stripes Show*, the National Cowboy and Western Heritage Museum, the grand reopening of the musical, *Oklahoma!*, the State Capitol dome dedication, the Olympic Festival, the Oklahoma Centennial Celebration, and the large Paul Moore sculpture of the Land Run of 1889.

Lee Allan is an exceptional Sooner who truly loves Oklahoma. He is Oklahoma's own Energizer Bunny.

—DAVID L. BOREN, *President,*
University of Oklahoma

Prologue

"Lee Allan, your daddy's not
ever coming home again!"*

To 12-year-old Lee Allan Smith, those words from
the lips of his mother in May, 1942, were, at first,
unreal. Lee Allan had begun the day as a happy seventh
grader at Harding Junior High School in Oklahoma
City, and was confused when the principal came to his
classroom to tell him his mother needed to talk to him
at home immediately.

A friend picked up Lee Allan and drove him the
mile or so to his home on Northwest 20th Street. He
had never been called home in the middle of a school
day—so he thought something must be wrong. Was
his mother sick? Was there bad news about his older
brothers who had joined the Army Air Corps? He had
heard his mother praying for his brothers, as war raged
in Europe and the Pacific. America had been thrust into
World War II only a few months before, when Japanese
airplanes attacked Pearl Harbor, Hawaii. Lee Allan
never imagined that his mother might have devastating
news about his father.

The horrible news was that William Ernest Smith
had been killed in an early morning hotel fire in
Wichita Falls, Texas. Smith and another man had

leaped to their deaths from the top floor of the seven-story Texan Hotel after flames engulfed the structure.

How could it be true? How could his father be taken so suddenly? He was a traveling salesman and was often gone for one week at a time—but he always came home on Thursdays. In summers, Lee Allan had accompanied his father on long trips to sell electric supplies to businesses in Oklahoma and surrounding states. They shared a love for baseball—although Lee Allan's mother discouraged her husband from taking their sons to Oklahoma City Indians games because she thought all baseball players were beer-drinkers and the game would have an adverse influence on her boys.

In the hours and days after receiving the news of his father's death, Lee Allan's world was turned upside down. Everything around him seemed to move in slow motion—it was like a movie with a sad ending. He saw a newspaper picture of the burned hotel and overheard someone reading a story about how ten other people had been injured in the fire. He had a mental picture of the hotel because he and his parents had stayed there just one month before on a visit to his brother who was stationed at Shepard Air Force Base.

Lee Allan did not fully understand the pats on the head and hugs he received from the scores of friends and family who came to the Smith home to convey their condolences. The adults were sweet and kind—but Lee Allan's dog, Lady, was the only one who seemed to really understand how bad he was hurting inside. Lady knew her master was sad—when Lee Allan sat under a tree in his backyard, she snuggled closer than normal.

To make matters worse, Lee Allan came down with the mumps the following day and had to be isolated in his bedroom. He even had to miss his father's funeral at First Presbyterian Church. His sister-in-law, Naomi "Nadie" Smith, stayed with him during the funeral and tried to reassure him that his mother, brothers, and other family members and friends would try to fill the void left by his father's untimely death. Nadie wrapped a cloth around Lee Allan's cheeks to quell the pain from the mumps. "I'm hurting, do something!" he pleaded.

As Lee Allan drifted into sleep, he wondered about his future. Would he and his mother be moving to a smaller house—would he be able to take Lady with him?

There were many unanswered questions that lay ahead for the Smith family of Northwest 20th Street in Oklahoma City.

chapter one

My brothers and my mother came to my rescue—
and helped fill the emptiness left by my father's death.

—LEE ALLAN SMITH

A LOVING FAMILY

William Ernest Smith at age 21. While still in Texas, Ernest worked with Earl Bentley, whose sons, Bill and John, became friends with Lee Allan in Oklahoma City many years later.

ee Allan Smith was born November 13, 1929, at St. Anthony Hospital in Oklahoma City. He was the youngest of four sons born to William Ernest Smith and Florence Phelps Smith.

Lee Allan's father, one of seven children, arrived in Oklahoma shortly after statehood from his home in Aubrey, Texas, where he was born in 1885. He was an accomplished musician and played in local bands. In 1914, he moved to Shawnee, Oklahoma, and met Florence Elizabeth Phelps, the only daughter of Elbridge Gary Phelps, who owned or managed several early-day newspapers in southeast Oklahoma, including weeklies in Shawnee, Seminole, Wewoka, Ada, and

The homestead of Lee Allan's paternal grandparents in Aubrey, Texas. Lee Allan's father, William Ernest Smith, commonly known as Ernest, was born there in 1885.

Tecumseh. Florence was born in Coldwater, Kansas, on March 15, 1890.

William Ernest, called Ernest by his friends, and Florence, commonly called "Flossie," were married on November 3, 1914, at First Presbyterian Church in Shawnee. The local newspaper had announced their engagement the month before. The wedding was a huge social affair in Shawnee. Hundreds of guests attended the event that featured a program of classical music, sharply dressed attendants, and glamorous women adorned in the finest gowns. Florence's only brother, Carl Phelps, was best man.[1]

Ancel Earp and Virginia Piersol also took part in the wedding ceremony. Earp was later one of the state's leading insurance executives. Piersol, the flower girl in the wedding, later married Luther Dulaney of Oklahoma City. Decades later, their two

RIGHT: Lee Allan's father, William Ernest Smith, was sales manager for Mideke Supply, an electric supply company. He represented Richard and Connover, Victor Electric Company, and other manufacturers.

BELOW: The Smith brothers and sisters in July, 1942. Left to right, Lena Smith Crawford, Jess Smith, Mae Smith Bryant, Coon Smith, Edith Smith Hodges, Neil Smith, and William Ernest Smith, Lee Allan's father.

sons, Tom and Dick, became close friends to Lee Allan.

Ernest worked for his father-in-law for awhile until he landed a job as a salesman for an electric supply firm in Oklahoma City. Florence gave birth to their first son, Donald Valdeen Smith, September 17, 1916. On November 23, 1918, a second son, Carl Phelps Smith, was born. Five years later, on July 29, 1923, still another son, Dale Donovan Smith, was born.[2]

The Smiths lived in a house on Northwest 23rd Street in Oklahoma City until Ernest was promoted to the position of territory salesman for Stratton-Tersegee, a regional electric supply firm. The family moved into a two-story home at 434 Northwest 20th Street, in a growing residential area two miles north of downtown.

Oklahoma and America were in a state of turmoil when Lee Allan was born in November, 1929. Only one month before, the stock market in New York City had crashed, signaling the beginning of the Great Depression, the longest and most severe economic downturn in modern history. Oklahoma suffered greatly. The state's economy was based largely on agriculture. With falling prices on livestock and grain, farm foreclosures were daily events.[3]

Banks failed, factories and stores closed, and millions of Americans were left jobless and homeless. Even though Ernest Smith was able to maintain his job during this time, the Smiths had to tighten their belts because his sales commissions were down—companies and cities and towns that normally bought electric supplies ran out of money.

Florence Elizabeth Phelps, Lee Allan's mother, at age 15 in Wewoka, Oklahoma. Her father managed the newspaper in Wewoka at the time.

Oklahoma City had enjoyed a decade of unprecedented prosperity before the Great Depression established its stranglehold on the state. The city had been "born grown," the result of thousands of residents claiming land along the North Canadian River in the Land Run of April 22, 1889. Oklahoma Station was the city's original name, literally blossoming into a city within hours after the federal government allowed settlers to compete for 1.8 million acres of unassigned land in central Oklahoma in the most spectacular land opening in world history.[4]

Just before Lee Allan's birth, oil had become the password of the Oklahoma City economy. On December 4, 1928, oil was discovered in the Oklahoma City field, the first time in America a significant oil discovery had been tapped within the city limits of a major city. Hundreds of jobs were created overnight—the population of the city increased by 10,000 within months.

Had it not been for the discovery, Oklahoma City's place in the Depression would surely have been worse. For four years after the beginning of the oil boom, Oklahoma City enjoyed more than $1 million per month in building permits and four public buildings were built in the current Civic Center area.[5]

Surrounded by benchmark events in Oklahoma City history, Lee Allan began his life during the coldest winter on record in the capital city. For six weeks in early 1929, temperatures hovered below freezing. Ice and snow halted construction jobs, although workers obtained temporary jobs for 50 cents an hour to shovel more than a foot of snow that stayed on city streets and sidewalks for weeks.[6]

At birth, Lee Allan Smith was christened Lee Allan Gary Smith. The Lee and Allan were names of his parents' favorite doctors. The Gary came from his grandfather, Elbridge Gary Phelps. Not long after this photograph was taken, Lee Allan's father sneaked him to the barber shop and had his curls cut off.

The four Smith boys in August, 1931. Left to right, Carl, Lee Allan, Donald, and Dale. Their dog, Lady, is at left.

One of the first things Lee Allan remembers about his childhood is his parents' emphasis on church attendance. His father and mother were deeply religious—he was Baptist, she was Presbyterian. However, both insisted that Lee Allan regularly attend Sunday school. He often walked to the First Presbyterian Church at Northwest Ninth Street and Robinson Avenue, before the congregation built a new sanctuary at Northwest 24th Street and Western Avenue.[7]

When Lee Allan's brothers came home on leave from military duty, the First Presbyterian pastor would visit the Smith home

Lee Allan and his first grade classmates at Wilson Grade School. Lee Allan is fifth from the right on the top row.

THE SPACER ◁19 40▷

PUBLISHED BY
4 COMRADES CLUB
FEBRUARY

Vol I No II

PRICE 3 CENTS

EDITOR . . . . EUGENE WHITTINGTON, Jr.
ASSISTANT EDITOR . . . . LEE ALLEN SMITH
REPORTER . . . . DICK VAN CLEEF
REPORTER & TREASURER . . . . BOBBY KEY
REPORTER . . . . DORIS JANE STEFFLE
REPORTER . . . . JOE KIRKPATRIK
PRINTER . . . . EUGENE WHITTINGTON

PROMOTION

You can't imagine that all but one of the little 3As were promoted to the 4B. The 6As are no longer 6As because they are all in High School and we miss them very much.

CUBS COLUMN

Den Two and Den Five had an assembly and a pantomime. Although Den Five won the prize for the funniest, Den Two did the best acting. The dens were only supposed to have a two minute act and Den Five had about a five or six minute act.

TRUE

That story about Eugene Whittington, Jr. is very, very absolutely inch for inch true. If anyone still has any doubt, here is Mr. Whittington's signature

Eugene H Whittington

And it's not a forgery.

newspaper edited while at Wilson school- (grade school)

FLASH !!!!!!!!!!!!!!!
FIRE

There was a fire in the boys basement at Wilson that created quite a sensation. The Junior Police all gathered around but they found out that the janitor had for some reason started a fire.

NEW PUPILS

There are two new pupils in Wilson. One is in the 5A and the other is in the 6B. The name of the one in the 5A is Priscilla (Prise) Morris. She has a sister in Harding that came from England too. The boy in the 6B is named Brandon Morse and came from Holland.

RIDDLES

1. What never answers questions but always has to be answered?

2. Who used a walking stick first?

3. Does the sea recognize you?

(Answers on Page 2.)

Lee Allan was the assistant editor of *The Spacer,* a mimeographed newspaper published by the 4 Comrades Club at Wilson Grade School.

to say a special prayer of thanksgiving for their safe return. It was a tradition that continued on many occasions when the Smiths were thankful for good fortune.

Lee Allan's parents provided a warm and loving home. His father was on the road much of the time, calling on businesses, farmers, and cotton gins in surrounding states. However, on weekends, Ernest gave full attention to his wife and baby son.

Lee Allan's two older brothers were out of the household by the time he began elementary school at Wilson Grade School. Dale, the closest brother in age to Lee Allan, was six years older.

Lee Allan liked the way his parents treated each other, with love and respect. When a teacher at Wilson School asked Lee Allan the name of his mother, he replied, "Dear." That is all he had ever heard his father call his mother.

Ernest's only habit that disturbed his wife was his smoking of cigars. Lee Allan picked up on that feeling and once said to his father, "Dad, just think how much money you could save and give to me if you quit smoking cigars." Ernest said, "Next time you open that glove compartment, money will be falling out." The next time Lee Allan climbed into his father's Ford automobile, Ernest had rigged the door of the glove compartment to fall open, dumping a bucket full of coins into Lee Allan's waiting hands.[8]

At Wilson Grade School, Lee Allan was outgoing and made friends with schoolmates. He learned the discipline to take naps from his kindergarten teacher, Mrs. Moore. Mrs. Dolliver, the librarian, taught Lee Allan how to properly hold and care for books. Mrs. Bernice Mock was the music teacher who taught

Lee Allan how to carry a tune. Mrs. Mock's husband, Fred, ran for governor of Oklahoma as a Republican, long before Republicans had a chance of becoming chief executive in the Sooner State. Mrs. Mock's son, Fred, Jr., was one of Lee Allan's good friends in grade school and throughout their lives.[9]

In the third grade, Lee Allan and his friend, Gene Whittington, as editors, published a neighborhood newspaper which told the latest gossip and covered sporting events at Wilson. Starting the

In February, 1942, Lee Allan, right, visited his brother, Donald, who had joined the Army Air Corps a few months earlier.

newspaper was Lee Allan's idea, largely because of the influence of his grandfather's newspaper career. A weekly edition was mimeographed at Whittington's father's insurance office and distributed to Wilson students.

When America entered World War II, the older three Smith boys joined the Army Air Corps. Donald and Carl achieved the rank of captain. Dale was a sergeant. Lee Allan knew his mother worried

Lee Allan in 1939 with his Collie, Lady. Note the rabbit cages in the background. The Smith boys always had pets in the backyard.

about his brothers. He couldn't wait to receive their letters from distant places like New Guinea and Italy.

While Lee Allan was still a student at Wilson, the Smith family moved to 720 Northwest 20th Street, the former home of aviation pioneer Tom Braniff, one of the founders of Braniff Airlines. Lee Allan's mother made a comfortable home of the two-story dwelling. It was in that home that Mrs. Smith and her sons mourned the death of her husband in May, 1942.

The neighborhood was filled with Lee Allan's friends. Across the street lived Richard Poole, later vice president of Oklahoma State University (OSU). Richard's mother sat on the front porch and played the piano, a delightful sound to accompany street games and shenanigans of the local boys.

Down the street was a man named Bill Harrah who had a basketball court in his backyard, a natural draw for neighborhood would-be basketball stars. One of the boys who played at Harrah's backyard court who became Lee Allan's good friend was Paul Hansen, later a basketball star at Oklahoma City Central High School and OSU. Hansen was a highly respected coach at Oklahoma City University and OSU.

Also in the neighborhood were Charlie Darr, who played football for the University of Oklahoma; John, Tom, and Jim Freeman; Sam Bounds; Noel Kruger; Robert McCormack; and John Shawver.

Lee Allan followed the footsteps of his brothers in active involvement in athletics. Carl was an excellent tennis player and Dale was an all around athlete who helped Lee Allan develop his skills as a baseball player. There was no doubt that baseball was not only the national pastime, but was Lee Allan's favorite sport. He loved attending Oklahoma City Indians games at Holland Field, later called Texas League Park, at Northwest Fourth

Curt Gowdy, right, was the voice of the Oklahoma City Indians in the late 1940s. Decades later, Lee Allan presented Gowdy with a football signed by the University of Oklahoma football team. *Courtesy University of Oklahoma.*

Street and Pennsylvania Avenue, just northwest of downtown Oklahoma City.

The ballpark was just more than a mile from the Smith house—Lee Allan often was allowed to ride his bicycle to a game and pay the ten cent admission price for an afternoon of dreaming about playing on the green grass of the manicured infield. He especially enjoyed exhibition games, when major league teams would appear in Oklahoma City before the regular season began.

The Indians were the top farm club for the major league Cleveland Indians. One of Lee Allan's favorite players was Al "Flip" Rosen who re-wrote the Texas League record book and then became a star infielder for the Cleveland Indians. After baseball, Rosen became president of the New York Yankees and later, general manager of the San Francisco Giants. In the 1990s, Lee Allan sent Rosen a book about Oklahoma and received a return letter in which Rosen said his playing time in Oklahoma City was a highlight of his baseball career.

Lee Allan hung around the ballpark so much that he came to know the radio voices of the Indians. Curt Gowdy, later one of America's favorite sportscasters, broadcast the Indians games in Oklahoma City on KOCY Radio, a 250-watt local station located at Plaza Court, an office complex between Lee Allan's house and the baseball stadium. Lee Allan was intrigued by Gowdy and other announcers recreating games that the Indians played in far off cities.

ABOVE: Lee Allan was 10 years old in 1939 when this photograph was taken with his brothers. Left to right, front, Lee Allan and Donald, and in back, Carl and Dale. Note the American flag pin on Lee Allan's lapel. Even at a young age, he was extremely patriotic, possibly because of his three brothers serving in the armed forces.

LEFT: The Smith home at 924 Northwest 20th Street in Oklahoma City.

Gowdy recalled, "Western Union made it possible. I used a small stick to strike a block of wood to emulate the crack of a bat. I had a picture of every Texas League ballpark in front of me so I could visualize 'being there.' I let my imagination soar."[10] Another baseball sportscaster that Lee Allan met at Indian games was Bob Murphy who later moved to the major leagues to call games for the Boston Red Sox and Baltimore Orioles before becoming the first announcer for the New York Mets. Both Murphy and Gowdy were later inducted into the broadcasting division of the National Baseball Hall of Fame.

After his father died, Lee Allan took a job delivering newspapers. Each morning he picked up bundles of *The Daily Oklahoman* near Kamp's Grocery at Northwest 24th Street and North Classen Boulevard. Lee Allan tried to arrive a bit early at the grocery store to feast on its famous pastries, especially cream puffs, before heading out to deliver papers in his neighborhood. In the afternoons, he delivered the *Oklahoma City Times*.

Only once did Lee Allan get into any trouble selling newspapers. When Italy surrendered in World War II, *The Daily Oklahoman* published a special edition. Lee Allan picked up extra papers and sold them at a higher-than-normal price to people waiting to catch the Interurban streetcar at the 17th Street station. The profit made from the paper route usually ended up paying for admission, hot dogs, and soft drinks at Oklahoma City Indian baseball games.[11]

The only person who tried to dissuade Lee Allan from playing baseball was his mother. Mrs. Smith's image of a baseball player was that of Babe Ruth—she

Broadway Avenue looking north in downtown Oklahoma City during Lee Allan's teenage years. There were several theaters downtown. Other frequent stops for Lee Allan and his friends were Marsh's Pig Stand at Northwest 18th Street and Broadway Avenue, Beverly's Chicken-In-The-Rough, and the Dolores Restaurant on Northwest 23rd Street. Dances were held in the Hall of Mirrors at the Civic Center and the Persian Room and the Skirvin Tower Hotel.

FRED ASTAIRE
GINGER ROGERS
ROBERTA
AND
BERRY
WATCHES
DIAMONDS

CRITERION

OF MUSICAL ROMANCES WITH FRED ASTAIRE AND GINGER
RENE DUNNE PLUS MILTON SLOSSER AT THE ORGAN

Lee Allan spent many Saturday afternoons watching
serial Westerns at the Victoria, Mayflower, or Plaza
theaters. Later he attended the "big movies" at the
Criterion, Midwest, Tower, Harbor, State, and Center
theaters in downtown Oklahoma City.

thought players were just a bunch of beer drinkers.[12] However, Mrs. Smith gave in and allowed Lee Allan to play baseball from an early age.

The Smith home was filled with music. Lee Allan's mother was a gifted pianist and had studied voice for 15 years. After supper many nights, Mrs. Smith would play the piano and Lee Allan would sing with her—everything from church hymns to the latest popular music like "Scarlet Poppies" and "Mulberry Bush." The march-beat hymn, "Onward Christian Soldiers," became Lee Allan's favorite song as a child.[13]

Lee Allan took piano lessons from a man named Herbert Ricker who lived a few blocks away. At first, Lee Allan did not like the idea of learning the piano under the tutelage of Ricker, although he was awed by his mother's proficiency at the keyboard. But after awhile, he began enjoying the lessons and actually performed at several recitals, including a well-attended event at Classen High School.[14]

Soon after the death of Lee Allan's father, the family moved to a two-story frame and brick house at 924 Northwest 20th Street.

Lee Allan's mother doted over her youngest son and tried everything in her power to make his life full and meaningful. "She lived by example and set a high moral standard for Lee Allan to observe," said Lee Allan's lifelong friend, Alfred Dewitt "Dee" Sadler, Jr.[15]

Mrs. Smith was buoyed by principles she had learned from her parents. Many years later, she told a newspaper reporter, "God was my burden bearer." Using constant spiritual tuning, she also lived by philosophies handed down from her parents— Don't let social standards ever pull you down—and—when you're lonesome, work![16]

The Smith's neighbor and jeweler B.C. Clark, Jr., knew the family well and remembered, "Mrs. Smith was a sincere woman who managed her budget closely to have extra money to give her sons a quality life. She always was talking about her family, especially her baby boy, Lee Allan. No conversation went very long without a mention of Lee Allan's latest successes."[17]

chapter two

Lee Allan had a magnetic personality, even as a teenager.
When he walked into a room at a party, everyone wanted
to talk to him. People did not call him by his full name—
they just said "Lee Allan," and we all knew who they were
talking about. —RANDY EVEREST

MAKING FRIENDS

Lee Allan's mother, Florence Smith, on the front porch of her home at 924 Northwest 20th Street. Lee Allan's dog, Lady, appears in most family photographs of the era.

M*aking friends came naturally to young Lee Allan.*
His outgoing personality and desire to have fun made him popular with both teenage boys and girls. He had a full head of flowing black hair that attracted the opposite sex. His ability to tell jokes and give humor to almost any situation made other teenagers want to be around him.

"No one was a stranger to Lee Allan," Richard "Dick" Ellis remembered, "Everyone was crazy about him—and he hasn't changed in 50 years!"[1]

To have extra money for social occasions and athletic events, Lee Allan worked a variety of jobs in high school. He performed odd jobs for the Kerr-Linn Oil

Company, a predecessor to Kerr-McGee Corporation, and was a file clerk for Ancel Earp Company, a large property and casualty insurance agency. The $10 to $15 he made each week allowed him to have plenty of spending money for weekend dates.

Lee Allan became an expert at selling Carnation ice cream to both children and adults when he pushed an ice cream cart twice a day from Broadway to Blackwelder avenues and up and down Northwest 20th, 21st, and 22nd streets. His boss, Ed Ferris, provided the cart that used dry ice to keep the ice cream cones and popsicles frozen until the sound of the bell on the cart lured customers from their homes.[2]

Lee Allan's mother strongly believed she should be at home when Lee Allan returned from school each day. She built a

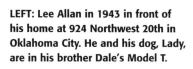

LEFT: Lee Allan in 1943 in front of his home at 924 Northwest 20th in Oklahoma City. He and his dog, Lady, are in his brother Dale's Model T.

BELOW: As a teenager, Lee Allan lived alone with his mother—his three older brothers were in the Army Air Corps, stationed at distant bases around the world.

small apartment onto the garage and rented it to adults she closely screened. The presence of other adults on the property provided a sense of additional security.

Following the death of his father, friends became even more important to Lee Allan. Friends such as Randy Everest, Jack Catlett, Leland Vance, Geneva Horstmeir, Fred "Tookie" Baker, G.W. James, Louie Trost, Stephen Chandler, Tommy Black, and John Trigg not only provided emotional support, they had cars—and Lee Allan did not. It was the primary way he could get to social and sports events even though he was sometimes allowed to drive his mother's 1937 Chrysler or, after World War II, her 1946 Ford purchased from Fred Jones Ford.

The Jones family lived three blocks from the Smiths and Lee Allan and his brother Dale were good friends with Fred Jones, Jr. Lee Allan enjoyed afternoons of playing badminton in the Jones backyard and talking with the beautiful Marylin Jones, who later married Sidney Upshur, Lee Allan's college roommate his freshman year in college.[3]

Randy Everest met Lee Allan in the seventh grade at Harding Junior High School. Both were members of the Hot Dogs, a social fraternity of about 30 boys who met at one of the members' homes each week and planned parties and dances. There were two fraternities and two sororities at Harding. Everest said, "Lee Allan was a little shy at Harding, but his personality blossomed as we entered high school."[4]

Lee Allan loved crackers, so fraternity chum Dee Sadler dubbed him "Krispy," a nickname that stuck at least through junior high school. Sadler remembered, "Every time he came to our house, he headed to the place where my mother kept the crackers. While we ate candy, he munched on crackers."[5]

Lee Allan was not the only one of the group of friends with a nickname. Edwin "Ed" de Cordova was called "Deedle," and Fred Mock, Jr., was referred to as "Ferdie."As Lee Allan followed his three brothers to Classen High School, his personality bubbled and he became one of the most popular boys on campus. Because of his mother's advice for him to respect authority and his elders, parents of other teenagers liked Lee Allan associating with their children. In fact, Mrs. Smith ushered him out the door to school each morning with the admonition, "Be a good American today!" or "Be good on the inside today!"[6]

Mary Katherine "Coca" Catlett Bell's younger brother, Jack Catlett, was one of Lee Allan's good friends who often invited him to stay for dinner. Coca and Jack's mother, Bertha, was from Louisiana and was an excellent cook. Lee Allan made himself at home with her chuck roast, chicken and dumplings, and chicken and noodles, all made from scratch.

Coca remembered, "We loved having Lee Allan over for family meals because he was so funny. He knew lots of clean jokes and was so optimistic about everything. At the end of the meal, we all felt better about our lives." Coca's parents considered Lee Allan a second son and believed his optimism, confidence, and work ethic provided a good example for their children.[7]

Lee Allan was an active member of a high school fraternity, Phi Lambda Epsilon, that provided opportunities for social activities and civic pride projects. The fraternity atmosphere created friendships that have lasted a lifetime. An example is Joe Dan Trigg, who shared membership in Lee Allan's fraternity at Harding Junior High School and Classen High School.

Trigg, who married Janice Guild in Lee Allan's class, said, "Even as a teenager, Lee Allan showed incredible leadership and people skills—traits that would lead him to great things for Oklahoma!"[8] Many years later, Lee Allan would work with Trigg and Pam Newby to promote Special Care, a facility for Oklahoma youth with special needs.

The Phi Lambda Epsilon chapter at Oklahoma City's Classen High School. Lee Allan is fourth from the left on the second row. Fraternity life was important to Lee Allan and his friends even in high school.

Lee Allan was the keeper of the fraternity scrapbook, a collection of photographs and mementos that won for him a first prize trophy and cash award at a national fraternity competition in St. Louis, Missouri.[9]

Before Lee Allan's senior year in high school, he and fraternity brother, Bill Shumate, worked for a fireworks wholesaler,

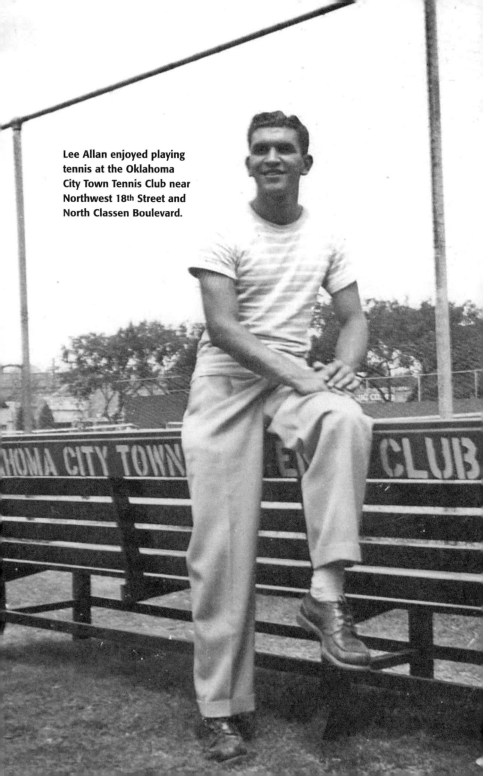

Lee Allan enjoyed playing tennis at the Oklahoma City Town Tennis Club near Northwest 18th Street and North Classen Boulevard.

Red Cannon, who supplied fireworks for retail stands from the first of June to after Independence Day. Lee Allan and Shumate built a fireworks stand from scrap lumber and began business in a high traffic location near Northwest 63rd Street and Kelley Avenue.

Lee Allan and Ed de Cordova also worked in Cannon's fireworks warehouse. Lee Allan occasionally drove a large panel truck to Dallas, Texas, and Denver, Colorado, to pick up a load of fireworks. Once, he had a blowout near Marietta, in southern Oklahoma, and barely escaped danger when the truck weaved through a maze of oncoming traffic. Lee Allan sat for an hour before he regained his composure and continued on his trip.[10]

Lee Allan's bubbly personality was used in a productive way when he starred as Wildcat Willie in a play titled *Wildcat Willie Buys a Bond* in Martha Downing's fifth-hour speech class at Classen High School. The play was presented to stimulate interest in buying war bonds. Lee Allan's mother was not overly fond of the role of Wildcat Willie. On occasion when she was disappointed in Lee Allan's conduct, she would refer to him as "Wildcat Willie."[11]

One of the times Mrs. Smith did not appreciate her son's actions was when he participated in walk outs at high school. On the Friday before the big football rivalry game each year with Central High School, Lee Allan and hundreds of students at Classen walked out of class and disappeared into the teenage haunts and neighborhoods around the school. Once, high school principal, C.E. "Pop" Grady, who Lee Allan revered, pulled him from beneath a nearby house where he was hiding. Lee Allan later roomed with Grady's son, Jim, at the University of Oklahoma (OU).[12]

No matter what Lee Allan did, his mother forgave him. When Lee Allan wrote a childish note to his mother, saying, "I am sorry for what I have done that was bad," Mrs. Smith responded, "You were never unruly or disobedient, but kind, sweet, clean, and happy." She signed the note, "Mother, with a depth of love."[13]

"Florence treated Lee Allan like a prince," remembered his sister-in-law, Nadie Smith, "and, in turn, Lee Allan was always good and faithful to his mother, just like his brothers who also worshiped her."[14]

Lee Allan made the Classen High School baseball team his senior year. He was a good outfielder and learned the game well from coaches Carole Smelser and Rex Erwin. He enjoyed

playing alongside Bill McGee, an all-state basketball player who attended college at the University of Notre Dame, Guy Fuller, and John Reddell, who played football and baseball at the University of Oklahoma.

Lee Allan never had a serious girlfriend in high school, although he dated several girls, including Phyllis Crowe and Joanne Deardorf. His first formal date was with Duane Colcord—a triple date with friends Dee Sadler and Leland Vance. Lee Allan always wanted to arrive early at Vance's house so he could visit baseball hall-of-famer Lloyd Waner, who lived next door. Waner was one of Lee Allan's heroes after becoming one of Oklahoma's most famous major league baseball players.[15]

Lee Allan often went stag to parties and social events, fully expecting to enjoy everyone's company. There was no shortage of fun for teenagers in Oklahoma City. On any given night, one could find Lee Allan and his friends at a movie, playing miniature golf, or drinking soft drinks at any of a half-dozen nearby teenage hangouts such as Marsh's Drive-In, the Pig Stand, or Blossom Heath. Occasionally, the group of friends would slip off to Snug Harbor, a nightspot with less than a stellar reputation, especially to parents.

Some of Lee Allan's companions were JoAnne Crawford, who married Blair Perkins, Barbara Brunner, Sue Caston, Jeannie Hoffman, Jeannine Eddy, and her twin brother Gene, Ann Tillman, Bill Blew, W. T. Hales, Nancy Nichols, Dave Amis, Jim Gonders, Ed Eskridge, Nancy Noftzger, Nate Graham, Pete Darcy, Mary Johnston, Pat Lester, Frank and Bill Robinson, Breene Kerr, Dick Workman, Thornton Wright, Charles Monnett, and Lee Sneed. In the summer, the action moved to Springlake Amusement Park in northeast Oklahoma

City, the Texas League Ballpark, or to Lake Overholser where dates could be taken on boat rides for a quarter.[16]

After four action-packed years, Lee Allan graduated from Classen High School in May, 1947. He was ready to spread his wings and continue his education in college.

chapter three

*In college, Lee Allan had a unique gift of organizing
special events—a glimpse of his later life.*

—EDDIE CROWDER

BOOMER SOONER

**Florence Smith,
Lee Allan's mother,
left, stands behind
her son at a
special mother's
tribute at the Phi
Gamma Delta
house. At right are
Bill Lockard and
his mother**

L *ee Allan Smith chose to enroll* at the University of Oklahoma in Norman because several of his high school fraternity brothers and good friends already had enrolled there. There were two other reasons Lee Allan selected OU—his mother urged him to continue his education and believed OU was the place for him to be, and he was a huge OU football fan.

The University of Oklahoma, established December 19, 1890, by act of the Oklahoma territorial legislature, began its storied history in a simple way. When classes convened in September, 1892, each student met with President David Ross Boyd to obtain a schedule and then was examined by a faculty of four. The entire course listing was printed on one page. Enrollment was a much more lengthy process in the fall of 1947 when Lee Allan arrived on the Norman campus.

As the beginning of summer before college classes began, Lee Allan and Jack Catlett hitchhiked to Guymon, Oklahoma, with visions of spending the entire summer and saving a bundle of cash. Lee Allan's brother, Donald, was a contractor/estimator on the new Guymon High School construction project and arranged for Lee Allan and Catlett to work. However, after the boys arrived, they discovered their "great" job for the summer was digging ditches.[1]

After one week of toiling long hours under the hot sun in the Oklahoma Panhandle, Lee Allan was offered a job as a water boy. Lee Allan did not think twice about reject-

ing the offer, because he would feel bad about Catlett still digging ditches. A few minutes after making the sacrifice for his friend, he looked up to see Catlett yelling, "Lee Allan, you want some water?" The story has been a source of laughter for decades.

Both boys, homesick and tired of the extreme manual labor, decided to return to Oklahoma City. They began hitchhiking together, but found they could catch rides better alone. They eventually made it back home, although their friends had never realized they were gone.[2]

Lee Allan's base of operations in Norman became the Phi Gamma Delta (Fiji) house at 119 West Boyd Street, adjacent to the OU campus. There was never any doubt that Lee Allan wanted to pledge the fraternity because he knew several of the upperclassmen. The OU chapter of

Phi Gamma Delta, Nu Omega, was one of 76 chapters of the national fraternity that was celebrating its centennial of service. The local group was installed in 1917 and was one of the more prominent fraternities on the OU campus.

Lee Allan's first roommate in the Fiji house was Sidney Upsher, who served as president of the local chapter. Lee Allan immediately established friendships with some of the older Fijis such as John Snodgrass, Richard "Dick" Clements, John Harrison, Joe Holmes, Gene Lewis, and W.A. "Dub" Henderson, all of whom were officers in the fraternity. Henderson was also Lee Allan's roommate. Other friends

Lee Allan, left, and Dick Ellis, with Patty and Susie Reily, at a party during their college years at the University of Oklahoma.

who became close to Lee Allan were Ed Moler, Dick Cain, Eddie Miller, Bill Lockard, Dick Dial, Jim Gorman, John Drake, Earl and Jerry Amundsen, Don Adkins, John Ross, and Forrest Mertz.[3]

Many of Lee Allan's older friends were military veterans, like Snodgrass who later became president of The Noble Foundation, one of Oklahoma's most prestigious philanthropic and research organizations. Snodgrass had served three years in the war arena in the Pacific before returning to OU.[4]

While in Norman, Lee Allan built a solid, lifelong friendship with OU football star Billy Vessels who won the coveted Heisman Trophy as college football's outstanding player in 1951. They double-dated and hung around together many weekends. After Vessels' death in 2002, his widow, Susie, wrote, "I am sorry that Billy is not here to contribute to the telling of Lee Allan's story. He and Lee Allan spent so much time together—they could read each other's minds."[5]

Lee Allan also became friends with Lee Stidham of Checotah and renewed his childhood friendship with Jay Carl Sanders and Richard "Dick" VanCleef, both of Oklahoma City. VanCleef had attended classes with Lee Allan since elementary school. Later came Dick "88" Ellis, a scholarship football player who lived at the Fiji house.

Lee Allan's magnetic personality drew new friends to him, both male and female. Soon, Lee Allan was

Lee Allan, second from right on second row, at a party at the Phi Gamma Delta house.

being called upon to organize social events. Dick Clements remembered, "He always thought on a grand scale, even if we were planning a party in the backyard of the fraternity."[6] Lee Stidham said, "Lee Allan's ability to dream, plan, and produce a great attraction developed while in school."[7] Once, Lee Allan temporarily took out windows of the fraternity house and built stairs into the backyard, so that guests could walk directly from the house onto the wooden floor for dancing.[8]

The Phi Gamma Delta basketball team, left to right, at back, Gene Heape, an OU football player and another of Lee Allan's roommates at the Fiji house, Bob Roop, and Rodney Lowery. In front, John Ross, Lee Allan, and Don Atkins.

Lee Allan, right, and Dick Ellis did their famous cigarette trick at fraternity parties and other social events.

To help finance his college education, Lee Allan worked as a sales clerk at Sturm's Clothiers on campus corner in Norman. The clothing store was owned by George Sturm who allowed Lee Allan to work up to 20 hours per week. Not only did the paycheck help, Lee Allan was able to dress in the finest men's clothing.

Lee Allan tried his hand as an entrepreneur and looked for ways to make additional money. He, Al Taylor, and Joe Crowder, the brother of OU football star Eddie Crowder, made hamburgers in the fraternity house and sold them after normal dinner hour for 20 cents each, a dime cheaper than

the going price at the Town Tavern, a popular college hangout down the street.[9]

To supplement his income from jobs, Lee Allan obtained a student loan from the Lew Wentz Foundation, and with the influence of Jack Catlett's father, Stanley B. Catlett, a loan from the Rapp Foundation. Later, when Lee Allan paid back the loan, the elder Catlett bragged on him. Catlett said 95 percent of students who obtained loans from the foundation never repaid them.[10]

Lee Allan and his friends frequented Jake's Cowshed. Left to right, Heisman Trophy winner and OU football All-American Billy Vessels, entertainer Lilly "The Cat" Christine, John Cox, and Lee Allan. Lee Allan, Vessels, and Dick Ellis often ate steak and eggs on Sunday mornings at the Monterrey Restaurant, nicknamed "The Mont," on Classen Boulevard in Norman.

On weekends when there were no fraternity parties, Lee Allan often went home to Oklahoma City to stay with his mother. During school breaks, he sometimes worked at the Sturm's Clothiers and Parks Clothiers in Oklahoma City. On occasion, south Oklahoma City political kingpin, J.D. McCarty, would hire Lee Allan to distribute campaign cards and place posters in the area for the election of Robert S. Kerr to the United States Senate. McCarty later successfully ran for the Oklahoma House of Representatives and later became Speaker of the House.

On visits to his mother, Lee Allan also looked up friends from high school who were attending other universities or had joined the military. Often the friends gathered at Up Town Pit, a barbecue restaurant and nightspot at Northwest 24th Street and North Walker Avenue, Vic 'n Honeys, the Branding Iron, or Tower Club.

Broadcast legend Danny Williams first met Lee Allan at the Up Town Pit, a popular gathering place for sports fans and personalities. Williams, who was already a local television star, remembered Lee Allan as "a bright, energetic college student who could make us all laugh into the night."[11]

One of the highlights of Lee Allan's college career was his friendship with OU President Dr. George L. Cross, a man in his early forties who already was making a huge impact upon Oklahoma's largest university. Lee Allan enrolled in a botany class taught by Dr. Cross and often talked football with him. Lee Allan saw as "brilliant" Cross' decision to hire Charles B. "Bud" Wilkinson as head football coach. Just as Lee Allan was beginning his college memories, the OU football team was beginning its road to national prominence, a trip made possible by Cross' leadership.[12]

Lee Allan's friendship with President Cross was fortunate, because occasionally the Fiji parties became rowdy and drew complaints that ascended up the bureaucratic ladder to the president's office. Lee Stidham, who had access to Cross, would explain to the president that all the party fun was innocent. Stidham's intervention prevented any punishment for the

In college at OU, Lee Allan, right, became friends with OU quarterback Eddie Crowder and his wife, Kate. Crowder later became an assistant football coach at OU and West Point and head football coach and athletic director at the University of Colorado.

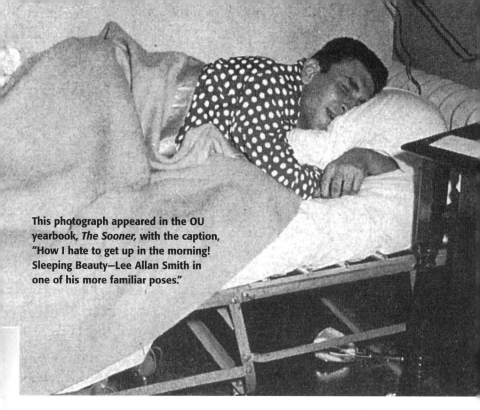

This photograph appeared in the OU yearbook, *The Sooner,* with the caption, "How I hate to get up in the morning! Sleeping Beauty—Lee Allan Smith in one of his more familiar poses."

LEFT: Lee Allan with Barbara Burke and Jack Catlett with Margo Marland at a fraternity party.

fraternity except for occasional minor restrictions.[13]

In the summer of 1948, Lee Allan worked in the Oklahoma County campaign headquarters of Robert S. Kerr in his quest for the United States Senate. In the headquarters in the Old City Hall Building at Broadway and Grand avenues, Lee Allan operated a mailing machine, sorted mail, and bundled campaign signs for distribution to neighborhoods.[14]

In his junior year, Lee Allan became Fiji social chairman and planned one of the greatest lineups of social events in OU fraternity history. Eddie Crowder, who starred

RIGHT: Left to right, at a Phi Gamma Delta reunion in 2002, Gene Heape, another of Lee Allan's college roommates; Dick Clements; Lee Allan; and Kenny Parker.

BELOW: Members of the OU chapter of Phi Gamma Delta in 1950. Lee Allan is fourth from the right on the third row.

as quarterback for the OU football team, said, "Every time I heard about what was happening at the fraternity house, someone was bragging about Lee Allan and his magical ability to plan the greatest events!"[15]

Crowder, two years younger than Lee Allan, recognized immediately Lee Allan's value as a friend and big brother in the fraternity. He said, "There was no question that Lee Allan cared for me like family. It gave great meaning to the term 'big brother.'"[16]

One of Lee Allan's responsibilities in his final two years of college at the fraternity was to serve as rush chairman. Crowder was a member of the detail that cleaned the fraternity house under Lee Allan's watchful eye. Crowder remembered, "He had a wonderful leadership style—he was always friendly and full of fun, not coercive."[17]

Lee Allan's efforts to give new fraternity members a good feeling about joining the group did not go unnoticed by Fiji alumni. After the 1951 Rush Week, A.F. Williams, owner of an Oklahoma City furniture company, wrote Lee Allan, "I have never seen a more conscientious job done for the fraternity both as rush chairman and as the man most responsible when the house was opened. I hope you will be able to pass on some of your energy and enthusiasm to the next guy."[18]

The Fiji list of committee chairmen in 1949-1950 was filled with future Oklahoma celebrities. In addition to Lee Allan as head of the intramural athletics committee, future commissioner of public safety and district judge, Joe Cannon, was in charge of freshman training, and William G. "Willie" Paul, later president of both the Oklahoma and American Bar Association, was co-chair of the publicity committee.[19]

Lee Allan became a popular master of ceremonies for campus events such as Sooner Scandals, an annual entertainment extravaganza. He also was a ready volunteer to work with other fraternities and sororities to plan events, including taking campus shows to entertain patients at Norman Municipal Hospital. His popularity allowed him to place second in the much-publicized Ugliest Guy on Campus (UGOC) contest. Frankly, Lee Allan was glad he did not win the contest. Surely, he thought, he was not the ugliest guy on campus.

Lee Allan missed most of one of his big annual fraternity parties because of a bet with Dee Sadler. On the day of the party, Lee Allan and Sadler were eating at a popular restaurant on campus corner. Lee Allan was enjoying his hamburger when he said, "Oh, I could eat a dozen of these things!" Sadler took him up on the bragging and promised to pay for the dozen hamburgers.[20]

Sadler left for class with Lee Allan about half way through the plate of hamburgers. An hour later, when Sadler returned, Lee Allan had eaten the remaining sandwiches, although he was, Sadler said, "green around the gills!" Lee Allan won the bet, but went to his room at the fraternity house in a nauseous condition.[21]

Later, Lee Allan was in Sadler's wedding to Beth Ann "Mike" Pound. After the ceremony in Ardmore, Sadler and his bride were taken to their well hidden automobile and headed south toward Texas for their honeymoon. However, as they approached the Texas state line, Lee Allan jumped up from under a pile of clothing in the back seat. Sadler pulled to the side of the road and Lee Allan waited for a ride from friends who were following the Sadlers in another car.[22]

Lee Allan took intramural athletics at OU to a new level. He put together sports teams and competitions in a professional manner, winning him the Intramural Manager of the Year

BELOW: Lee Allan served on the board that controlled intramural sports at the University of Oklahoma. The board was made of coaches and junior and senior intramural managers. Seated, left to right, Mrs. Loyce Watson, secretary; Lee Allan's longtime friend, Bill Lawrence; Dewey "Snorty" Luster; and Max Parks. Standing, Paul V. Keen, chairman; Jerry Foster, Lee Allan, Monte Moore, Bob Wertz, Alex Aven, and Henry Presson. Moore, the son-in-law of OU men's basketball coach, Bruce Drake, later became the voice of the Kansas City and Oakland Athletics major league baseball team.

LEFT: The Fiji team of Lee Allan and Hal Wolfe won the 1950 OU intramural badminton doubles. Left to right, runners up Bob Daubert and Bill Lawrence, Lee Allan, and Hal Wolfe. Lee Allan also did well in the singles competition until he was eliminated by Scooter Hines, who, at 5 feet six inches, starred for the OU basketball team. Lee Allan scored the first nine points of the set—but never scored again.

Award. He worked with Paul V. Keen, director of intramural athletics and former OU wrestling coach, and former football coach Dewey "Snorter" Luster, who coached the OU boxing teams.

Because of his outstanding work, Lee Allan was selected to serve on the board that oversaw intramural competition among 5,000 OU students on 12 softball diamonds, 12 touch football fields, 21 tennis courts, 6 handball courts, 6 horseshoe pits, 1 track, and 1 indoor swimming pool. Running so many intramural events was more than a full-time job for Lee Allan. To give more interest in tournaments, and make Fijis proud even when they did not win an event, he often raised money from fraternity alumni in Oklahoma City to buy second place

ABOVE: Lee Allan looked forward to fraternity parties—the good time and the ample supply of food. Left to right, Margo Marland, Lee Allan, Mary Bartleson, and Lee Stidham. Mary and Lee were later married. Mary's sister, Jeanette, married J. Howard Edmondson who was elected governor of Oklahoma in 1958.

RIGHT: At a formal party are, left to right, Dick VanCleef, Lee Allan, Betty Jo Ingram, and Phyllis Patterson. Lee Allan had no serious girlfriends in college although he enjoyed dating girls like Ingram, Ann Daniel, and Virginia Schleppey of Tulsa and Nancy Puckett of Amarillo, Texas.

trophies—the Department of Intramural Athletics only provided trophies for the winners in each competition.[23] The training that Lee Allan received from Keen on how to organize sports competitions would be used throughout Lee Allan's life.

Although Lee Allan had sporadically played baseball since junior high school, he tried out for the OU baseball team his senior year. The team was coached by the legendary Jack Baer who had coached the Sooners to a national baseball championship in 1951.

Lee Allan made the squad, but could not play because of a bad knee and because Coach Baer did not think Lee Allan was as good a player as Lee Allan thought he was. Baer was kind enough to appoint Lee Allan as student manager and allowed him to travel with the Sooners to away games. Lee Allan was given a half scholarship by Baer and Gomer Jones that, most importantly,

allowed him to take his meals at Jefferson House. Eating at the athletic dormitory was convenient because Lee Allan lived across the street in an apartment with Dick Ellis and Jennings Nelson, another OU football player.[24]

During meals, practices, and on baseball team trips, Lee Allan enjoyed friendships with many of the players, including John Reddell, Buddy Leake, Ken Stonecipher, Bill Harrah, Orville Rickey, Carl Allison, and Buster Cloud, whose son, Jeff, serves as a member of the Oklahoma Corporation Commission.

Lee Allan's best buddy on the baseball team was Roger Wich. On one trip to play the Kansas University Jayhawks in Lawrence, Lee Allan and Wich slipped out of their rooms and went to the Kansas University Fiji house. It was there that Lee

The 1948 men of University Sing, a choral group at the University of Oklahoma. Lee Allan is seventh from the left on the back row.

Allan met Dean Smith who became one of college basketball's greatest coaches at the University of North Carolina. Ever since the chance meeting at the Fiji house, and the subsequent serenading of girls at a nearby sorority house, Lee Allan and Smith have been good friends.[25]

All male students at OU were required to enroll in military classes as part of their college curriculum. Lee Allan chose the Reserve Officers Training (ROTC) program of the United States Air Force (USAF). At the end of his four years of service, he

Lee Allan, at left on the back row, was the student manager of the OU baseball team during his senior year at the university. At top right is coach Jack Baer. Carroll Swickey, said Lee Allan was one of the best baseball players he ever saw on the diamond. Tom Brett said, "Wow, how he could hit the ball!"

was commissioned a second lieutenant in the USAF Reserve. In order to receive the commission, Lee Allan had to commit to serve two years on active duty.

Lee Allan dropped out of college for a semester, working at Sturm's Clothiers and Parks Clothiers in Oklahoma City. He returned to school and officially graduated with a Bachelor of Business Administration degree in June, 1953. With his college career behind him, he was ready to don his Air Force uniform and begin active duty.

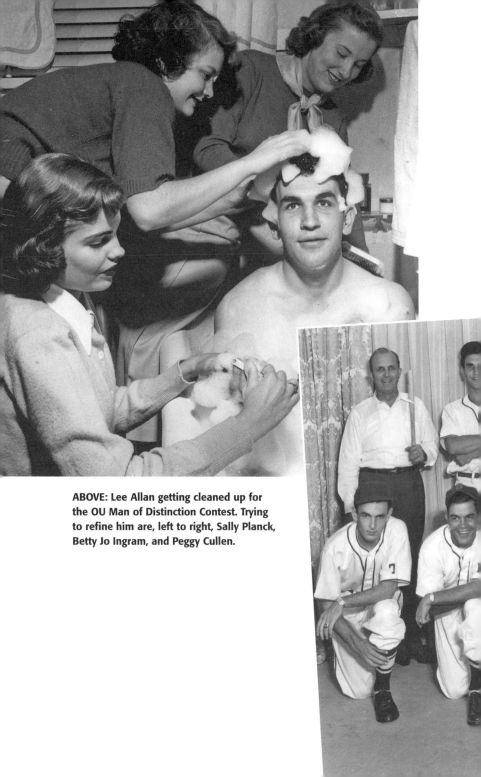

ABOVE: Lee Allan getting cleaned up for
the OU Man of Distinction Contest. Trying
to refine him are, left to right, Sally Planck,
Betty Jo Ingram, and Peggy Cullen.

BELOW: Lee Allan, second from the left on the back row, played softball in a summer league of teams made up of mostly Sigma Chi members. He had been recruited after hitting a home run against the Sigma Chi team in a fraternity championship game. The Sigma Chi team was sponsored by the Aero Blind Company, owned by Stanley Brown's father, Gus. Lee Allan juggled practices and games with his job at Sturm's Clothiers. Star pitchers included Reece McGee and Dick Conklin, two of the best pitchers around, and Maury Flynn, Billy Lawrence, Russell Brown, Mac Dunning, Bob West, Sam Brunell, and Ray Plumb.

chapter four

*Whenever you're on my base, you will follow my
Lieutenant Smith!*

—Wheelus Air Force Base commander,
COLONEL ROLLEN H. ANTHIS

TO THE SHORES OF TRIPOLI

**Lee Allan in
Paris, France, on
leave. During his
Air Force assign-
ments in Europe
and Africa, he
was able to visit
many famous
cities while on
short leaves.**

T*o begin his Air Force career,* Lee Allan was
required to attend a two-week Air Force orien-
tation at Lackland Air Force Base in San Antonio,
Texas, in March, 1953. After being issued uniforms and receiving limited basic training, he was
shipped to an Information and Education School
at Fort Slocum in New Rochelle, New York. The
Air Force had granted his wish to become a Special
Services officer, a sports and entertainment planning specialist.[1]

After the training at Fort Slocum, Lee Allan was
ordered first to Vienna, Austria; then to Munich,

Germany; and finally to Tripoli, Libya, on a two-part mission—to coach baseball and basketball and help put on United Service Organization (USO) and other entertainment shows for servicemen.

Lee Allan spent only two months in Vienna and was transferred to Munich as part of the 317th Troop Carrier Wing. After a short time in Germany, he was assigned to

ABOVE: Lee Allan, center, assists Colonel Loren Cornell, left, in the presentation of an award to an airman in Vienna, Austria.

UPPER LEFT: Lee Allan, left, and Walt Yowarski, an outstanding University of Kentucky football player, at the Hofbrau House in Munich, Germany, where they were stationed before Lee Allan was transferred to North Africa. Yowarski was the most valuable player in the 1950 Sugar Bowl when OU was beaten by the University of Kentucky.

LEFT: Lee Allan, right, visits with a Russian soldier in September, 1953, when the Soviets handed over control of the international sector in Vienna, Austria, to the United States. Control of the sector rotated among the four occupation powers—the United States, Britain, France, and Russia.

the headquarters unit of the 1603rd Air Base Group in Tripoli. His job was deemed important by his superiors—sports and entertainment activities were vital to maintain high morale among troops stationed in the isolation of the North African desert.

The Air Force recognized that military men and women and their spouses had an unusually tough time coping with the extreme heat and frequent ghiblis that rolled across Libya from the desert to the sea in the summer months. During a ghibli, that was nothing more than heavy, hot, sandy winds, temperatures often reached 135 degrees. When asked where the term "ghibli" originated, locals invariably answered, "Somewhere south of here—probably in hell."[2]

Lee Allan was stationed at Wheelus Field, the largest American air base in the world. After the United States took over the base after World War II, it became the busiest military air base, in terms of air traffic, in the world. Planes took off at the rate of one per minute.[3]

Wheelus was located about five miles outside Tripoli, the ancient capital of Libya, located on the Mediterranean Sea. The city had become famous in the Marine Corps Hymn, "From the halls of Montezuma to the shores of Tripoli," because of an 1804 Marine raid on a pirate stronghold in the city.[4]

Wheelus, occupying 16,000 acres fronting the blue Mediterranean, was actually owned by the Libyan government, but leased by the United States military. Airmen were careful not to call the installation a base and were repeatedly reminded that Libya was not an occupied country and that the United States was a guest of the Libyan government.

When Lee Allan arrived in Libya, he immediately discovered the challenge of providing entertainment and sports activities for the military men and women stationed there. One of the biggest on-base attractions was a sprawling beach beside the Mediterranean that Lee Allan promoted as "a military Coney Island." Lee Allan also sold his superiors on the idea to make available to airmen who needed rest and relaxation more Military Air Transport Service (MATS) flights to Athens, Greece; Rome, Italy; other exotic cities in Europe; and the Holy Land.[5]

Wheelus Field was commanded by 37-year-old West Point graduate Colonel Rollen H. Anthis, from El Reno, Oklahoma, who welcomed Lee Allan's suggestions on how to improve morale among the officers and airmen whose only way to get away from Libya was by airplane—it was like living on a scorching island.[6]

The police in Tripoli, Libya, granted Lee Allan a Libyan driver's license. He needed the license to drive a blue Volkswagen Bug he purchased for $700 in Tripoli.

As in many situations with people throughout his life, Lee Allan had a "connection" with Colonel Anthis. In addition to the commander being from Oklahoma, Lee Allan had dated his relative, Anna Claire Anthis, of Muskogee, Oklahoma, while at OU. During Lee Allan's first official meeting with Anthis, who later was promoted to brigadier general, he discovered the Oklahoma connection and used it to his benefit. Once when an escort officer became upset with Lee Allan for taking his entertainment troupe to the officers' club, rather than just entertaining enlisted men, Anthis listened to the complaint and said, "Whenever you are on my base, you will follow my Lieutenant Smith!"[7]

ABOVE: Lee Allan riding a camel in front of the officers club at Wheelus Field outside Tripoli, Libya. Lee Allan is holding a pack of Camel cigarettes, hoping he could earn some extra income by sending the photograph to the cigarette manufacturer. He never heard from the tobacco company.

Lee Allan and his guides on a trip to the Jordan River. He was able to use leaves to visit The Holy Land and many cities in Europe.

BELOW: Lee Allan thought the desert around Tripoli, Libya, was a stark contrast to the tree-lined streets where he grew up in Oklahoma City. In this photograph, he poses in front of Roman ruins at Sabratha outside Tripoli.

In addition to coaching baseball teams at Wheelus Field, Lee Allan played outfield on one of the teams, the Nomads, that traveled to the United States Air Force Europe championship in 1954.

In 1986, Lee Allan was able to pay tribute to Anthis, who retired as an Air Force brigadier general, for kindness shown more than three decades before in Africa. Lee Allan asked Anthis to sit at the head table at an Oklahoma City Chamber of Commerce luncheon honoring Admiral William J. Crowe, Chairman of the Joint Chiefs of Staff.

Using the skills developed managing an intramural athletics program in college, Lee Allan organized a highly successful system of sports activities for men and women at Wheelus. As soon as Lee Allan arrived in the summer of 1954, he developed

The Wheelus Nomads made it into the top elite eight of the 1954 USAFE baseball championship. Lee Allan is at left on the top row.

leagues and schedules, convinced groundskeepers to improve sports venues, and used the base newspaper, the *Tripoli Trotter*, to publicize sporting events. His congenial way with reporters resulted in comprehensive coverage of sports competitions.

Lee Allan led the construction of a golf course, with hard sand greens. Playing on sand did not inhibit hundreds of officers and airmen who took advantage of using the ghibli wind to correct their hooks and slices.

Lee Allan spent a lot of time coordinating visits of entertainers to Wheelus. The USO brought The Tops in Blue show, with comedian Jerry Van Dyke and the Harmonicats, and boxer Slapsie Maxie Rosenbloom. Lee Allan was able to coordinate

Wheelus Field commander, Colonel Rollen H. Anthis, right, presents Lee Allan a trophy after the Wheelus Nomads played in the 1954 USAFE baseball championship. The trophy paid tribute to Wheelus teams that excelled in baseball and basketball.

the visit of several entertainment troupes to the air base each month, an accomplishment noticed by Colonel Anthis.

Don Klosterman, another Special Services sports and entertainment lieutenant, became one of Lee Allan's best military friends. Klosterman had played one year of professional football for the Los Angeles Rams, a team he would later serve as general manager. Lee Allan and Klosterman used leave time to travel to many countries in Europe. Both enjoyed golf and other sports and took advantage of sporting opportunities in England, Holland, Denmark, Greece, Turkey, Austria, Germany, Cyprus, Syria, and Israel. They had been stationed together at Munich, Germany, before Lee Allan was reassigned to Libya. In Munich, Lee Allan and Klosterman occupied plush quarters normally occupied by Air Force doctors.[8]

Lee Allan coached basketball and baseball teams at Wheelus. As a 24-year-old first lieutenant, he played outfield on the Wheelus Field Nomads baseball team he coached with Frank Smorch of Flint, Michigan. After a 13-7 season record, the team played in the United States Air Force Europe (USAFE) baseball championship at Rhein-Main Air Base, Germany, in August and September, 1954. Rhein-Main, who won the championship, was led by Lowe "Junior" Wren, a former football star and record holder at the University of Missouri, who became good friends with Lee Allan. Wren later played professional football with the Cleveland Browns.

Lee Allan used any holiday to plan special events for officers and airmen. On July 4th, 1954, he organized watermelon eating contests, sack races, ping pong tournaments, wheelbarrow races, and potato obstacle races on the Wheelus beach, followed by an Air Force band concert and a fireworks display from an offshore crash boat.[9]

Lee Allan, left, and Sergeant Jack Kelso examine a small Dorcas gazelle, a gift from Libyan King Idris to the Wheelus Field zoo, founded by Lee Allan as an attraction for men and women stationed at the isolated air base. The zoo experience in North Africa helped Lee Allan decades later in his work with the Oklahoma City Zoo.

Lee Allan was sitting next to Colonel Anthis when it was time for the fireworks display, made possible by huge boxes of fireworks Lee Allan had purchased on a trip to Rome. As the band played the "The Star Spangled Banner" and huge spotlights were turned on the American flag that waved proudly from a crash boat offshore, the first wave of fireworks "was a dud—nothing but smoke." Anthis turned to Lee Allan and said, "Lieutenant Smith." Fortunately, within a few moments, the smoke cleared and a beautiful display of fireworks began. Lee Allan remembered, "It was a scary moment!"[10]

One of Lee Allan's most unique promotions at Wheelus was his zoo. At the request of King Sayyid Muhammed al-Idris (King Idris), the ruler of Libya, Lee Allan managed to gather animals from the desert around the base to set up a small display—the first zoo in Libya. Soon, people from far and wide, military and civilian, came to visit the animal collection. King Idris presented a rare Uaddam to the zoo in the name of the people of Tripoli. A Uaddam is the colloquial name for the Dorcas gazelle, a graceful antelope that lived in the arid regions of North Africa. Lee Allan had no choice but to elevate his animal collection to zoo status. He said, "When the king gives you an animal, you must open a zoo!"[11]

Lee Allan organized the first Ghibli Bowl football game for Thanksgiving Day, 1954. When he presented the idea to have football teams from other air bases play the contest at Tripoli Stadium, an outdoor facility in downtown Tripoli, Colonel Anthis did not think Lee Allan could pull it off. However, with the help of other Special Services officers, Lee Allan convinced officers at Rhein-Main and Ramstein air bases in Germany to join the Thanksgiving celebration. Another Oklahoma connection helped seal the deal—the commanding general of USAFE was William H. Tunner, whose wife was from Oklahoma.

King Idris and other Libyan officials were among the 4,000 spectators at the Ghibli Bowl. Palm trees and donkeys were among the few reminders that the game was being staged anywhere but the United States. Half an hour before the game, stadium seats were filled and incoming spectators began looking for spots on the hot sand to sit and wrap in blankets. Even in the desert, Thanksgiving Day was chilly.[12]

The game brought Lee Allan back together with airmen with which he had previously been stationed. John Netoskie, a football hero at the University of Kentucky, and Jim "Gabby" Hook, a University of Missouri gridiron star, played in the game. Later Netoskie and Lee Allan took the same ship home to America.

Teen-aged girls from the Wheelus Base High School served as majorettes in the Ghibli Bowl, tossing silver sticks into the air, and as cheerleaders for both teams, the Rams and Rockets. A three-piece band played the National Anthem and fight songs throughout the contest. The Rams won the game and received a trophy from John L. Tappin, the American ambassador to Libya.[13]

The Ghibli Bowl was so successful, Lee Allan received commendation letters from his commanders. Colonel Anthis wrote, "This affair, in addition to making our Thanksgiving Day complete, gave our Libyan friends an opportunity to get a first-hand glimpse of a typical American athletic contest and its associated activities."[14]

Lee Allan's group commander, Colonel B.G. Dilworth, said, "This fine entertainment…will go far to help in our most cordial relations with our neighbors in this foreign soil." Dilworth said the Ghibli Bowl was probably one of the largest crowds ever assembled at a sports contest in Libya. He wrote, "Their satisfaction and praise makes our efforts worth while."[15]

In March, 1955, Lee Allan completed his two years of active military duty and headed home aboard the USS *Upshur*. After a rough trip across the Atlantic Ocean, he purchased a brand new, 1955 chartreuse and cream Chevrolet Bel Air in New York City, and drove non-stop to Tulsa, Oklahoma, where he rested a night before driving home to Oklahoma City, and reporting for duty in the United States Air Force Reserve. He was honorably discharged in July, 1961.

With his military service behind him, Lee Allan needed a job. Hopefully, he could use the skills developed in college and in the Air Force.

AFE COMMANDERS

ABOVE: Lee Allan, right, and Brigadier General William H. Tunner watch the first ball being thrown out at the USAFE baseball championship. In 2004, a half century after the event, Lee Allan was visiting with his friend, Jean Gumerson, of Oklahoma City, who was talking about her friend, the widow of an Air Force general. Ironically, Lee Allan and Jean, who worked on many civic projects together, discovered their lives had crossed paths with the Tunner family decades apart.

RIGHT: Libyan King Idris joined other Libyan officials and military leaders in the VIP section of Tripoli Stadium on Thanksgiving Day, 1954, for the Ghibli Bowl football game.

chapter five

Lee Allan was such a successful salesman, he sold the Gaylord family on the idea of making him, at age 28, assistant manager of the number one radio station in the state.

—DICK CLEMENTS

LOOKING FOR A JOB

Edward L. Gaylord,

Edward L. Gaylord, the son of Oklahoma Publishing Company chief Edward K. Gaylord, assumed control of OPUBCO's broadcasting operations. He and Lee Allan forged a close friendship that lasted nearly half a century until Gaylord's death in 2003.
Courtesy Oklahoma Publishing Company.

Lee Allan moved in with his mother at 924 Northwest 20th Street in Oklahoma City and began looking for a job. He assumed he could land a position with an oil company because many of his friends were working for some of the many oil companies that called Oklahoma City home. However, either the oil companies were not hiring, or they had no positions that remotely interested Lee Allan.

Lee Allan naturally looked toward broadcasting or advertising agencies for employment. He had been a proficient salesman at men's clothing stores and a successful promoter on three continents.

To have some money coming in, Lee Allan began selling stocks and bonds for a financial adviser, H.I.

Josey. But Lee Allan did not feel comfortable selling stocks and bonds and stayed with the job only two months.

He turned down an insurance sales job from his old friend Rollin B. "Ike" Smith but stayed busy by working part time at Parks Clothing Store. At least he was earning money while he developed a resume and began contacting broadcast stations for interviews.[1]

He asked for a job as a salesman at KWTV, the local CBS affiliated television station in Oklahoma City—but he received no return phone call after the interview. He discovered a fraternity brother, John Moler, was manager of WKY-Radio, Oklahoma's first radio station. But the "connection" hurt him, because Moler was concerned that people might think he hired Lee Allan as an advertising salesman just because of their fraternity connection.[2]

The door at WKY opened in the summer of 1955 because of Lee Allan's job at Parks Clothing Store. Carter Hardwick, the station's sales manager, became a good clothing customer of Lee Allan. After their acquaintance turned into a friendship, Hardwick told Moler, "I have found a young man who would make a great salesman!" Moler then had an excuse to hire his fraternity brother, Lee Allan.

Lee Allan jumped into his new job with the same enthusiasm that had made his college and Air Force days so successful. His personality allowed him to walk into a business and overwhelm a potential customer on the good things that could happen if the business bought advertising on WKY-Radio.

Lee Allan was honored to work for WKY. The station went on the air in 1922 in the living room and garage of the home of its founder, Earl Hull. The station was able to broadcast a few hours per week from profits made from selling radio receivers.

Radio was a novelty—when WKY began broadcasting, there were less than 30 radio receivers in Oklahoma City.[3]

The Oklahoma Publishing Company (OPUBCO), publisher of *The Daily Oklahoman* and *Oklahoma City Times* and headed by Edward King "E.K." Gaylord, bought the station in 1928 for $5,000. The station became an affiliate of the National Broadcasting Company (NBC).[4]

The Oklahoma Publishing Company had recently ventured into television broadcasting. WKY-TV began relaying network programs from NBC in 1952. E.K. Gaylord's son, Edward Lewis Gaylord, supervised the broadcasting operations. When WKY-TV purchased color cameras, it became the first

WKY-TV purchased this mobile unit to broadcast live from sports events such as University of Oklahoma football games. It was also used to cover the devastation caused by the 1947 tornado that swept through Woodward, Oklahoma. *Courtesy Oklahoma Publishing Company.*

Lee Allan was chairman of the Association of Metropolitan Stations (AIMS), a group of broadcasting executives in Canada and the United States.

LEFT: Oklahoma Governor J. Howard Edmondson, left, poses with Lee Allan and the gubernatorial proclamation naming Lee Allan chairman of the state's Fly the Flag Week in 1959.

Lee Allan, left, at the inauguration of J. Howard Edmondson as governor of Oklahoma in January, 1959. Behind Lee Allan, WKY-TV's Tom Paxton is interviewing Oklahoma City Mayor Allen Street. The cameraman is Bob Rodkey.

independently owned television station in the nation to broadcast local programs in color. WKY-TV bought the sixth RCA color camera—the first five color cameras were owned by NBC in New York City.[5]

In 1951, WKY Radio and WKY-TV began broadcasting from new facilities on Britton Road in north Oklahoma City. WKY-TV became the first television station in the country to establish a meteorology department.[6] The station depended heavily upon local programs.

A frequent visitor to Oklahoma City was Don Klosterman, who Lee Allan met in the Air Force. This photograph was taken while Klosterman was on his way to play for the Toronto Argonauts of the Canadian Football League. Klosterman, who was paralyzed below the waist in a skiing accident, later was general manager of the Dallas Texans, the Kansas City Chiefs, and Baltimore Colts. He was probably best known as general manager of the Los Angeles Rams of the National Football League. In Los Angeles, Rams' owner Carol Rosenbloom called Klosterman the "assistant owner." *Courtesy Oklahoma Publishing Company.*

Danny Williams arrived in Oklahoma City from San Antonio, Texas, in 1950 and began hosting radio programs. In 1954, he moved to WKY-TV as the host of *The Adventures of 3D Danny*, a children's show intended to compete with KWTV's *Mickey Mouse Club.* The program, the idea of Hoyt Andres, assistant general manager of WKY-TV, was extremely popular. Most children raised in the era never forgot Williams in his role as superintendent of the Space Science Center. Viewers joined the Universe Science Corps and received thunderbolt patches and

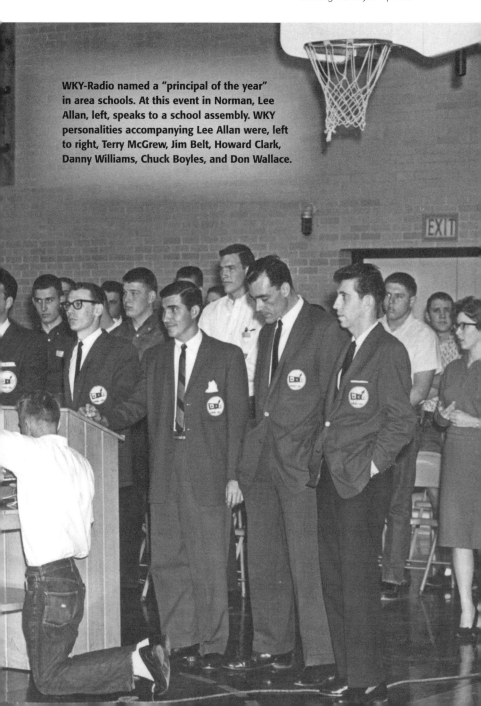

WKY-Radio named a "principal of the year" in area schools. At this event in Norman, Lee Allan, left, speaks to a school assembly. WKY personalities accompanying Lee Allan were, left to right, Terry McGrew, Jim Belt, Howard Clark, Danny Williams, Chuck Boyles, and Don Wallace.

interplanetary money. At about the time Lee Allan joined OPUBCO's broadcasting family, WKY-TV began airing *The Foreman Scotty Show*, where eager children in the audience visited the Circle 4 Ranch and watched the cowboy star chase villains.[7]

Lee Allan impressed his superiors at WKY-Radio by becoming one of the top producers in the radio sales department. When Hardwick left WKY-Radio in early 1956 for a management position at a Gaylord station in Montgomery, Alabama, Lee Allan became radio sales manager. Two years later, Moler took a job in New York City and Lee Allan was promoted to assistant manager of WKY-Radio. Dick Clements remembered, "We were shocked—but not surprised. It had been a meteoric rise for the young man who came home from the Air Force just looking for a job."[8]

Lee Allan also impressed young Jim Greenwald, a salesman at Katz, a New York City-based company that represented WKY-Radio and WKY-TV with national advertisers. The Gaylord broadcasting operation was Katz's second client. Greenwald, who eventually became the president of Katz, said, "From the first moment we met, I knew Lee Allan would quickly move up the management ladder. He grasped the idea of how promotion and radio advertising worked hand in hand. He could convince the most conservative businessman to spend his last dollar on 30-second radio spots."[9]

Lee Allan's popularity in his new position at WKY-Radio caught the eye of J. Howard Edmondson, the young, handsome Tulsa County Attorney who was among eight candidates in 1958 running for the Democratic nomination for governor of Oklahoma. Lee Allan and Edmondson, another Phi Gam, became close friends during the campaign. As assistant manager of the state's leading radio station, Lee Allan was a valuable advisor on advertising.[10]

Edmondson won the Democratic nomination by defeating Midwest City, Oklahoma, builder W.P. "Bill" Atkinson, in the "Prairie Fire" campaign. Edmondson came from the rear of the pack to overtake older and more experienced politicians to become Oklahoma's youngest governor ever. He and the new lieutenant governor, George Nigh, were in their early thirties and were featured in an article about future American leaders in *Life* Magazine.

Lee Allan was full of ideas about how to make WKY-Radio better. General Manager Norman Bagwell spent most of his time managing WKY-TV and left budget and programming decisions and other day-to-day operations of WKY-Radio up to Lee Allan.

Radio was changing. After World War II, the precise formats of radio dramas and live entertainment were giving way to programs of more recorded music. However, WKY-Radio continued to carry news and dramas from NBC and filled its early morning hours with detailed news, farm, and weather reports. Then, Lee Allan and program director, Danny Williams, changed the station's format to rock and roll. KOCY-Radio had introduced rock and roll to Oklahoma City, but WKY-Radio soon took over the number one position in ratings. Lee Allan remembered, "It was Danny who was the genius who made the rock and roll format work in Oklahoma City."[11]

With Williams in the all-important morning time period, WKY-Radio put together a team of disc jockeys that could induce the younger generation to listen to popular music, mixed with a strong presentation of local news. Williams became the most popular disc jockey in Oklahoma City—he once finished

first in a Coca Cola contest of the most liked and most disliked category. It was a gamble for Lee Allan, because many stations across the country had failed in transitioning local television stars into radio personalities.[12]

Lee Allan's favorite restaurant in Oklahoma City was Vic 'n Honey's. In this photograph, he poses with owner, "Honey" Boheim and Gloria Winters, who appeared as "Penny" on the *Sky King* television show.

Lee Allan and Williams began listening to audition tapes from disc jockeys wanting to fill the time slots in the WKY-Radio schedule. They hired Chuck Dunaway, Howard Clark, Chuck Boyles, Don Wallace, Terry McGrew, Johnny Dark, and Ronnie Kaye to spin records during a spectacular decade of popularity for WKY-Radio.

Dunaway, a popular disc jockey in Houston, Texas, flew to Oklahoma City to have dinner at Jamil's Steakhouse with Lee Allan and Williams. Dunaway showed up for the interview in a shiny silk suit he had bought for the occasion. Williams remembered, "He looked like a successful disc jockey, so we hired him!" Dunaway eventually posted record numbers in monthly ratings.[13]

Lee Allan also beefed up the news operations of WKY-Radio by hiring Bob Flournoy as news director. Flournoy began a tradition that vaulted the WKY-Radio news team to the top of the market for years.

Lee Allan, the consummate promoter, made WKY-Radio "show-biz." He convinced Edward L. Gaylord to invest in a mobile broadcast studio with a traveling light sign above it. WKY disc jockeys played basketball games for charity with high school teams and anyone who could suit up five players. Lee Allan remembered, "It was real show business—getting our name in front of people."

In addition to his more than full-time job of making WKY-Radio a success, Lee Allan had other interests. He served as a Purple Legionnaire, a chapter adviser to his fraternity chapter at OU, and became an usher and later a deacon, elder, and member of the board of trustees at First Presbyterian Church.

Lee Allan continued to support University of Oklahoma athletics and rarely missed football and basketball games on the Norman campus. In late 1958, he was at an OU basketball game when he noticed a beautiful, dark-haired girl in a black sweater. Lee Allan nudged his friend, Fred "Tookie" Baker, and said, "Can you believe how beautiful that girl is?" At the time, Lee Allan had no idea that the girl, DeAnn Dudenhoeffer, a senior beauty queen from Grandfield, Oklahoma, would quickly become the love of his life.

chapter six

*It was the luckiest moment of my life when I spotted DeAnn
in the middle of a group of students at the OU field house.
I thought she was the most beautiful woman I had ever seen.*

—LEE ALLAN SMITH

DEANN

**DeAnn
Dudenhoeffer
while a student
at the University
of Oklahoma. For
Christmas, DeAnn's
parents gave her a
new Chevrolet that
was delivered by
Chevrolet dealer
and dear friend Jack
Jones who dressed
up like Santa Claus
and knocked on
DeAnn's door. It was
a great surprise.**

eAnn Dudenhoeffer was born in the charm-
ing southern Oklahoma town of Grandfield
on November 5, 1936. Her father, William Joseph
"Bill" Dudenhoeffer, born in St. Louis, Missouri, in
1907, raised wheat, cotton, and cattle on land around
Grandfield. Her mother, Thelma Webb Dudenhoeffer,
born in Grandfield in 1909, worked for Bell Oil
and Gas Company until son Bob was born in 1945.
DeAnn's paternal grandparents, Frank and Elizabeth
Dudenhoeffer, had met and married in St. Louis,
Missouri, but moved to the fertile land along the Red
River shortly after Oklahoma became a state.[1]

DeAnn, the only girl in the Dudenhoeffer family
for many years, won the hearts of her grandparents
and spent much of her childhood playing with her
Dudenhoeffer cousins, Philip, Art, Clay, Frank, and
Mike, around the rambling farm house on the land
north of Grandfield. DeAnn was seven years older

111

than her only brother, Robert Stephen "Bob" Dudenhoeffer, born in 1945. Bob died in 1967.[2]

DeAnn and her family lived in town. While her mother was working, she was cared for by her maternal grandmother, Katherine "Kitty" Webb, who lived with the Dudenhoeffers.

Grandmother Webb played a significant role in the development of young DeAnn. One of DeAnn's earliest memories is of sitting on her grandmother's lap in a rocking chair on the front porch and receiving huge hugs from her. Family was important to the Dudenhoeffers. They spent Christmas Eve at their own home, but always moved the celebration the next day to the elder Dudenhoeffer farm.[3]

DeAnn's maternal grandmother, Katherine "Kitty" Dudley Young Webb lived with DeAnn's family and stayed with DeAnn while her mother worked for Bell Oil and Gas Company in Grandfield. DeAnn loved her Grandmother Webb, a true Southern lady from Kentucky with a wonderful disposition and loving ways.

DeAnn liked life on the farm. She was excited when her grandfather bought baby chickens that huddled around her

LEFT: DeAnn's grandparents, Frank and Elizabeth Dudenhoeffer, moved to Oklahoma in 1907. Frank's father, Franz Dudenhoeffer, was born in Germany in 1846 and emigrated to America in 1872. He drove the first wagon and team across the newly-completed bridge across the Mississippi River at St. Louis, Missouri, in 1874. In 1884, he homesteaded land at Lindsay, Texas, near Gainesville, and applied for American citizenship three years later.

feet for warmth. She enjoyed riding horses and swimming in the stock pond fed by a windmill that brought cool water from beneath the sun-parched fields. In the barn, she and her four Dudenhoeffer cousins swung from the end of a long rope to land on soft bales of hay.[4]

DeAnn looked forward to staying all night with her Grandmother and Granddaddy Dudenhoeffer and driving into Grandfield on Saturday nights to shop and visit with neighbors. Before she was a teenager, DeAnn was allowed to drive her grandmother's shiny red car into town because Mrs. Dudenhoeffer did not drive. DeAnn simply got behind the wheel and figured how to make the car go. She was so short—she had to look through the steering wheel to see where she was driving.[5]

Later, driving without a license turned sour on one occasion. DeAnn was required to ask her parents' permission to drive their vehicle to town. But one afternoon, her parents were asleep. Without permission, DeAnn and a friend drove to a fishing hole, looking for boys on which they had a crush. On a washed-out road, DeAnn turned her father's new pickup truck over on its side. One of the hardest things she ever had to do in her life was to tell her father she had wrecked his pickup. She never drove family vehicles again without permission.

Grandmother Dudenhoeffer was a classic German cook. The family benefited from fruits, vegetables, pickles, chow-chow, and other foodstuffs she canned for consumption in the long, cold winters. DeAnn's mother tried to pass on her excellent seamstress skills and later gave her tips on how to cook after she was married.

Fortunately, DeAnn was not required to do much work on the Dudenhoeffer

RIGHT: DeAnn's parents, Thelma and Bill Dudenhoeffer, lived in Grandfield, Oklahoma, after they were married.

DeAnn and her mother, Thelma Dudenhoeffer, in later years. DeAnn recognized that her mother was not only book smart but had extraordinary common sense.

farm. Once when she drove a wheat-filled truck from the field to a nearby grain elevator, her father found her parked alongside the road watching turtles swimming in a small body of water. Mr. Dudenhoeffer went looking for her and said, "What in the world are you doing here? You're supposed to be unloading wheat!" That was about the extent of DeAnn's farm-work experience, although she operated a snow cone stand for thirsty farm workers during harvest.[6]

Bill Dudenhoeffer and his two children, Bob, left, and DeAnn in 1940 in the Wichita Mountains. Mr. Dudenhoeffer thought DeAnn could do no wrong. He was always in his daughter's corner.

Fishing was a "get-a-way" for DeAnn and her father who liked to travel to Lake Texoma for a weekend of sand bass angling. DeAnn also enjoyed the company of cousins on her mother's side of the family. Grandmother Webb would take DeAnn, by train, to Wichita Falls, Texas, to visit DeAnn's favorite aunt who she called "Aunt Sister," and her three daughters, Zorene, Janice, and Marilyn. Aunt Sister was a school teacher, loved history, and spent hours telling old family stories. DeAnn and her mother also made trips to see family in Fort Worth, Texas, where she played with cousins Mike, Ken, and Tommy. Other Texas cousins were Robert "Sonny Boy" and Margie Jo.

DeAnn always planned to go to college so she worked at the two drug stores in Grandfield at the same time in her senior year of high school to earn extra money. She worked after school and some Saturdays at the soda fountain. She also worked at a TG&Y store, a clothing store, and in the school office. She always liked to stay busy.[7]

DeAnn was active in the Methodist Youth Fellowship at the Grandfield Methodist Church. Earlier in life, she had attended both the local Catholic church and First Christian Church. When First Christian closed, she became a Methodist.

In high school, she played basketball, was a majorette in the band, president of the Future Homemakers of America, queen of the Future Farmers of America, football queen, yearbook editor, took piano lessons, and participated in class plays and speech contests.

DeAnn graduated from Grandfield High School in May, 1954, and enrolled as a business major at the University of Oklahoma. She pledged Chi Omega and moved into the sorority house near the OU campus. She wanted to be a high school business teacher.

On weekends, DeAnn often took girlfriends to visit her aunt, uncle, and cousin in Oklahoma City. Tom, Connie, and Betty

Jean Webb lived in a two-story house near a park. DeAnn and her friends were treated like princesses and were allowed to sleep in Aunt Connie's guest bedroom with lots of pillows stacked on an eggshell silk bedspread.

DeAnn was an active college student. She regularly attended McFarland Methodist Church in Norman, appeared in Sooner Scandals and University Sing several years, and did volunteer work with children afflicted by cerebral palsy. She was proud of her parents and loved their visits on Mom's Day and Dad's Day. DeAnn went to most home basketball and football games and was selected as a Sooner Yearbook Beauty.

She was pinned to another OU student when she was spotted by Lee Allan at the OU basketball game in December, 1958. Lee Allan was very interested in her and asked friends to "check her out." He was not deterred by the fact she was regularly dating another young man. DeAnn remembered, "Lee Allan kept calling me even though I did not know him—and I was going with someone else! DeAnn thought, "Who is this guy anyway?"[8]

In the summer, DeAnn and her boyfriend parted company at about the time one of her friends was asked to set up a blind date for an "older" man named Lee Allan Smith, who was seven years older than DeAnn. When the friend asked DeAnn if she knew Lee Allan, DeAnn laughed. The friend encouraged DeAnn to go on the blind date with Lee Allan, although DeAnn had decided he was "a little unique because he keeps calling me to say, 'I saw you at the ballgame!'"[9]

Before the blind date, DeAnn had no idea what Lee Allan looked like. But she thought he was very handsome when he and Dick Ellis showed up to take her and her friend to dinner at the Officer's Club at South Base on the OU campus. Lee Allan, as a veteran, had admission rights to the club which served fine meals.

DeAnn dated Lee Allan, but not exclusively, for the next few months. She thought he was "pretty special," but was wondering when she might ever spend time with Lee Allan alone—his good friend Fred "Tookie" Baker always seemed to be around during their infrequent dates.[10]

DeAnn graduated from OU in May, 1959, and took a job with a law firm in Denver, Colorado. Her parents were against the idea, but Lee Allan's brother, Dale, and his wife, Ann, helped DeAnn find an apartment for her and Sharon Weeks, a friend who also intended to move to Denver.[11]

DeAnn began dating a law student who worked as an assistant in the law firm. Lee Allan missed DeAnn very much and actively began to pursue her. He occasionally "just showed up" at DeAnn's job or house, or in the middle of lunch. DeAnn would have no idea he was in town and never figured out how he would know exactly where she was eating.

Lee Allan depended upon his brother and sister-in-law to "check up" on DeAnn's life and the status of her relationship with the law student. Eventually Lee Allan and DeAnn talked and decided she should move back to Oklahoma City—a decision that greatly pleased both Lee Allan and DeAnn's parents.[12]

DeAnn began working for an Oklahoma City architectural firm, Hudgins, Thompson, and Ball, and moved into an apartment on a side street southwest of Kamp's Grocery Store on North Classen Boulevard. Lee Allan introduced her to a girl who became DeAnn's roommate. DeAnn said, "There was no question Lee Allan was trying to manipulate the situation. He talked me into moving back to Oklahoma!"

By Christmas, the relationship grew serious. DeAnn's mother and father were a little concerned that Lee Allan was seven years older, but their doubts faded when they met him and were charmed with his wit and obvious love for their daughter. DeAnn does not remember Lee Allan formally proposing. She remembered, "He just showed up at my apartment with a tray of rings from B.C. Clark!" DeAnn accepted the obvious suggestion of matrimony.

They were married on February 13, 1960, at First Methodist Church in Grandfield. The Reverend Joe Carson, the local Methodist pastor, officiated at the wedding ceremony. Lee Allan's brother, Dale, was best man, and Earlene "Dean" Walker, a high school friend, was DeAnn's maid of honor.

The newlyweds drove to New Orleans, Louisiana, for their honeymoon, but DeAnn came down with a horrible cold. Lee Allan called her parents and said, "She's sick! I'm bringing her home!" Lee Allan drove through a nasty storm but arrived at home where Mrs. Dudenhoeffer nursed her only daughter back to health. Lee Allan and DeAnn moved into a home owned by his brother, Carl, on Northwest 17th Street.

DeAnn's first meal for Lee Allan was anything but successful. She placed a pot roast in a roaster and followed her mother's instruction on the exact temperature. What she did not remember was how long her mother said to cook the roast. She was so proud when Lee Allan came home. However, her pride was diminished when she removed the roast—it was black and about half the size it had begun. Neither Lee Allan nor DeAnn could cut the roast so it ended up in the trash. DeAnn did not cry—but the story has been a great source of laughs for decades.

ABOVE: Lee Allan, right, was 30 when he and DeAnn were married in 1960. His best man in the wedding was his brother, Dale, left.

RIGHT: Lee Allan and DeAnn were married at the First Methodist Church in Grandfield, Oklahoma, February 13, 1960, and spent their honeymoon in New Orleans, Louisiana.

RIGHT: Left to right, DeAnn's parents, Bill and Thelma Dudenhoeffer; DeAnn; Lee Allan; and his mother, Florence Smith, at Lee Allan and DeAnn's wedding in February, 1960.

BELOW: Lee Allan and DeAnn in front of his brother's house on Northwest 17th Street in Oklahoma City. This is where the newlyweds made their first home.

For Lee Allan and DeAnn, their first year of marriage was busy. She gave birth to their first daughter, Stephanie DeLee, on a frigid, wintry night, December 30, 1960. During the pregnancy, she and Lee Allan decided to build a new house in the Wileman Addition in northwest Oklahoma City. Lee Allan and attorney George Short, and his wife, Margaret, bought adjacent lots on Riviera Drive in the addition southeast of May Avenue and Northwest 63rd Street.

The Smiths and the Shorts even used the same builder, Jack Clark, and moved into their new homes in early 1961. In 2005, they were still neighbors, **George and Margaret Short have lived next door to Lee Allan and DeAnn on Rivera Drive in Oklahoma City for more than 40 years. This photograph was taken on a trip the Smiths and Shorts took to New York City.** and intended to be neighbors for eternity. George Short said, "After we lived beside each other for 20 years, we decided to purchase neighboring burial plots at Roselawn Cemetery."[13]

DeAnn holds her first daughter, DeLee, in August, 1961. DeLee was only a few months old when the family moved into a new home at 6033 Riviera Drive in Oklahoma City.

chapter seven

WKY had a great tradition—but it was our people who made us number one!

—LEE ALLAN SMITH

BROADCASTING EXECUTIVE

Oklahoma City Mayor James Norick presents Lee Allan and WKY Radio an award for promoting employment of the handicapped. Ever the master salesman, Lee Allan, closely monitored his advertising sales staffs for both radio and television.

Lee Allan's lifelong love for America led him to be appointed by Governor J. Howard Edmondson as state chairman of the "Fly the Flag Week" in May, 1961. To aid in the program to encourage Oklahomans to fly the American flag, Lee Allan enlisted the help of chambers of commerce, public schools, Boy Scouts, Girl Scouts, women's clubs, civic organizations, newspapers, and radio and television stations.

The threat of communism was raising public awareness of the value of freedom. In his executive proclamation designating the week of May 1-7, 1961, as "Fly the Flag Week" and appointing Lee Allan as chairman of the event, Governor Edmondson said, "Our precious heritage of freedom must not, for an instant, be taken for granted since

the guardianship of freedom is the personal responsibility of each citizen of our great state of Oklahoma and our mighty nation."[1]

He also headed the Youth Fitness Jamboree held on the OU campus before an exhibition professional football game between the Dallas Cowboys and Baltimore Colts. Youngsters from around the state participated in fitness tests conducted in connection with President John F. Kennedy's Youth Fitness program. Lee Allan used his contacts to convince two-time Olympic decathlon champion Bob Mathias to be master of ceremonies for the event. Oklahoma sports heroes such as Marques Haynes, Allie Reynolds, Frank Kellert, Tommy Tatum, Ernie Vossler, and Betsy Cullen appeared on the program with Lee Allan.

Lee Allan expressed his concern about the future of his hometown by actively participating in worthwhile civic endeavors. When the Oklahoma City 89ers minor league baseball team opened play, Lee Allan became a one-man season box seat and

Popular singer and Oklahoma native Roger Miller, left, dons an Oklahoma Broadcasters Association crown at the OBA convention in 1965. Lee Allan was elected president of the organization that year. The crown was made by Doyle Glazier, a genius in the art department at WKY-TV.

Lee Allan appeared in a television commercial for a local automobile dealership.

season ticket campaign salesman. When he sold more season tickets than anyone else, he asked that his prize of a free trip to Houston, Texas, to see the 89ers' parent major league club, the Houston Colts, be kept secret and be given to the second highest producer. Oklahoma City Chamber of Commerce manager, Stanley Draper, Jr., wrote, "Lee Allan was the winner by a huge margin, but he did not want the credit for the sales he made. It was known to only two people that the award and recognition was given to the other person."[2]

Lee Allan was an active member of the All Sports Association, which produced the All College Basketball Tournament. He single handedly raised the operating budget for Oklahoma City Beautiful one year and worked on numerous projects of the Sports & Recreation Committee of the Oklahoma City Chamber of Commerce.[3]

In the 1960s, WKY-Radio and WKY-TV dominated the Oklahoma City market. Lee Allan had proven wrong those critics who had said the popularity of television would mean the death of radio—that any change in format from the dramas of "Amos 'n Andy," "One Man's Family," and "Young Widder

Lee Allan, points to Oklahoma in a 1966 C & H Sugar promotion. Left to right, Dahl Brown, representing C & H, Lee Allan, and WKY personality Danny Williams.

Brown" would result in loss of advertising. In fact, Lee Allan's installation of a Top 40 rock and roll music format at WKY-Radio was a huge success—advertising revenues rose at unprecedented rates.[4]

Lee Allan's theory was that stiff competition of television and other Oklahoma City radio stations made WKY-Radio better. He said, "It's like the four-minute mile. Roger Bannister might

never have reached that milestone unless he had other runners at his heels."[5]

Lee Allan liked to tell potential advertisers, "We've lost half our audience in the last 20 years! We've dropped to 50 percent of the listeners in town—down from 100 percent when WKY was the only station on the dial."[6]

In 1965, Lee Allan was elected president of the Oklahoma Broadcasters Association (OBA), the organization that represented the state's radio and television broadcasters. His constituents re-elected him for another term in 1966.

For the campaign to increase public service by broadcasters, the Oklahoma Broadcasters Association was given a special Code Authority Award of Merit by the National Association of Broadcasters (NAB) in 1963. Lee Allan traveled to the NAB convention in Chicago to receive the award on behalf of Oklahoma broadcasters.

As president of OBA, Lee Allan encouraged member broadcast stations to emphasize service to local communities by presenting public service announcements and programs. He told the 1966 OBA meeting, "The only way to keep federal control of broadcasting at a minimum is for us to be good public servants—to become involved in our communities and promote good programs and worthy causes. If we don't provide better public service, the government will try to tell us how to do it."[7]

On February 1, 1966, Lee Allan was named assistant general manager of both WKY-Radio and WKY-TV and began splitting his time between the radio and television sides of the Gaylord family stations in Oklahoma City. Tom Parrington became manager of WKY-TV. Lee Allan managed the day-to-day operations of WKY-Radio.

Lee Allan continued to believe that a strong news department was critical to maintaining high audience ratings. He added Bo Nance, Jim Palmer, and Ernest "Jim" Istook to the radio news staff. Istook later was elected to the United States House of Representatives from Oklahoma's Fifth Congressional District.

Ernie Shultz was the WKY-TV news director, following in the steps of Dick John and other anchors who had won the hearts of central Oklahoma residents for years. The station was a training ground for newsmen and women who eventually landed network or top ten market jobs. An example is Bob Dotson, who began as a news reporter for WKY-TV in 1969. He later began a stellar career with NBC. In 2005, he was a special correspondent for the *Today* Show.

Other news reporters who perfected their skills at WKY-TV were George Tomek and Jack Ogle. Joe Jerkins was a talented and brilliant program director, assisted by Bill Thrash. Art Garretson, Nick Panos, Art Atcheson, Don Webb, and Hudson Shubert were excellent sales personnel.

Lee Allan knew first hand how important sports news was to radio and television audiences in Oklahoma. He remembered, "Oklahomans loved their sports and it was serious business to produce a professional and accurate sports report."[8] Ross Porter, the son of a Shawnee, Oklahoma, newspaper publisher, became the state's leading sports anchor before moving to Los Angeles, California, to become one of the West Coast's best known sports broadcasting personalities and voice of the Los Angeles Dodgers. He was chosen several years to broadcast the World Series on NBC.

In 1966, Bob Barry, sales manager and part owner of KNOR Radio in Norman, began appearing as a weekend sportscaster. Barry was the voice of the University of Oklahoma Sooners. He later became sports director of WKY-TV and dominated annual competitions for Broadcaster of the Year in Oklahoma.

In the summer of 1966, the decision was made to produce all WKY-TV programs in color. Many changes had to be made—more lighting and air conditioning, and new sets for the studio. To complicate the change, the station had to produce local programs with just three color cameras, until others could be ordered and integrated into the operation. Because so few shows were broadcast in color, retailers in Oklahoma City had reported slow sales of color television sets. However, after the announcement was made that WKY-TV was going full color, sales skyrocketed. Retailers could not stock enough color sets to meet consumer demand.

To compete with *American Bandstand* on ABC, and locally on KOCO-TV, WKY-Radio disc jockey Ronnie Kaye began

Lee Allan's love for baseball and Oklahoma culminated in his close friendship with the state's greatest baseball star, Mickey Mantle. In 1965, Mantle finished second only to fellow New York Yankee Babe Ruth in a national poll of recognizable names in major league baseball history.

RIGHT: Because of Lee Allan's high profile job, he came in contact with leading entertainers. At a Chicago, Illinois, restaurant in 1965, Lee Allan, left, talks with comedian Red Skelton, second from left. Relationships forged in the 1960s allowed Lee Allan to bring superstars to Oklahoma City for the next 40 years. Later, Skelton was the headliner at the opening of the Stars and Stripes Park.

BELOW: WKY-TV sportscaster Ross Porter, left, at his going-away party after accepting a job as the voice of the Los Angeles Dodgers. Looking on are Lee Allan, center, and Norman Bagwell. Porter went to the NBC-owned and operated television station in Los Angeles and excelled as a sportscaster on the West Coast and nationally.

hosting a Saturday afternoon teen dance show, *The Scene,* on WKY-TV in 1966. Kaye was already a popular local disc jockey who invited teens strutting the latest fashions and dancing the latest dances to appear on the program.[9]

Lee Allan entered the restaurant business in the 1960s. Along with friends Sed Kennedy and Bill Shumate, he opened the Across the Street Restaurant on Boyd Street on campus corner across from the OU campus in Norman. The highly successful restaurant featured ordering from telephones installed in booths—an idea Lee Allan had seen in the Resi Restaurant and nightclub in Berlin, Germany, during one of his baseball trips in the Air Force.[10]

Lee Allan and his partners remodeled a building that had been used as a grocery store. Interior decorator, Tom Hoch, added his genius to the design of the restaurant. The partners added two additional Across the Street locations in Oklahoma City before selling the enterprise.

The Across the Street menu reflected its location adjacent to OU. A pizza burger with Sooner Sauce was 55 cents; a Big Red steak, served with salad, Suzy-Q potatoes, buttered bun, and Sooner Sauce was $2.95; and the Lady Red, smaller steak was only $1.95. A small coke was 10 cents.[11]

Later, Lee Allan, along with Jon Cain, G.T. Blankenship, Ed Quigley, and Ed de Cordova, opened Daddy's Garage, a unique restaurant on North Western Avenue in Oklahoma City. The restaurant featured old automobile parts—the salad bar was located under a used hood. Lee Allan got the idea for the restaurant on a trip from Tulsa to Oklahoma City. He took old US-66, rather than the Turner Turnpike, and began buying radiators, fenders, and license plates to adorn the walls of Daddy's Garage that was located on the present site of the Metro Restaurant.[12]

America was a divided country in the late 1960s. The unpopular Vietnam War spawned protests on college campuses and huge anti-war demonstrations in the major cities of the country.

Lee Allan had never minded people expressing their opinions on controversial issues—but when college students began burning American flags in protest of the war—he was very unhappy.

His friend, Ed de Cordova, remembered, "When the hippies started burning the flag, it really got under his skin."[13]

From the time he was a small boy, Lee Allan was seriously patriotic. He and his brothers had served proudly in the American military. At every special occasion, Lee Allan displayed the flag and promoted patriotism among school children. He knew he had to do something to counter the unpatriotic scenes he saw on the nightly news.

During a Sunday morning sermon at First Presbyterian Church in early 1969, Lee Allan was challenged by a sermon on patriotism by The Reverend Ralston Smith. Pastor Smith talked about how citizens ought to express patriotism and love of country, especially in the face of so much negative publicity about flag burning and the Vietnam War.[14]

Lee Allan's mind began to wander. He frankly tuned out the minister as he thought of ways he could organize a citywide event to pay tribute to America. After church, he shared the idea with his friend, attorney William "Bill" Robinson, who remembered, "I just smiled at him, knowing that he had gone over the edge."[15]

That night, Lee Allan called Oklahoma City public events director Dan Saunders and reserved the State Fair Arena for the next Fourth of July. Lee Allan had no specific plans—he just believed in his heart that his fellow citizens would support an Independence Day celebration.[16]

He began talking with friends and formed the Oklahoma City Association of Broadcasters to throw its support behind the idea. A non-profit corporation was organized to handle income and expenditures for producing a special Fourth of July show, buying and distributing flags for automobile radio antennas, and creating a city park with a patriotic theme.[17]

chapter eight

Lee Allan loves his country, state, and city more than anybody I know.

—ED DE CORDOVA

STARS AND STRIPES

Bob Hope shakes hands with admiring fans at Will Rogers World Airport in Oklahoma City. Lee Allan is at his side. On Hope's first visit to Oklahoma City, Lee Allan was asked to schedule a massage for the star at midnight. Lee Allan called upon friends at the YMCA to fulfill Hope's request. *Courtesy Oklahoma Publishing Company.*

T he Oklahoma City Association of Broadcasters settled on the name *Stars and Stripes* for the entertainment extravaganza that Lee Allan began planning. He knew he needed a military band but had no idea how to book such a performance. He started at the top by calling the White House. Lee Allan remembered, "I didn't talk to the president, but I did make contact with an aide from Oklahoma."[1]

The call to the White House resulted in a commitment from the Strategic Air Command Band, commanded by Jimmy Roland, and considered one of the finest musical organizations in the United States Air Force. It was another example of Lee Allan's Oklahoma connections—Roland was from El Reno, Oklahoma.

Lee Allan was off and running. He could hardly sleep—ideas for making the *Stars and Stripes Show* a huge success were constantly entering his mind. Within weeks he contracted a bevy of personalities to appear in the show. Former Miss Oklahoma Anita Bryant was a featured star.[2]

Also appearing in the show was Elk City, Oklahoma, native Jimmy Webb, the brightest young song writer in the country, who flew in for the show from Las Vegas with singer Connie Stevens where they had been performing at the Desert Inn.

In a college classroom Webb had written the melody to "Up, Up and Away," and followed with many hit songs recorded by Glenn Campbell, Andy Williams, Frank Sinatra, Richard Harris, Ed Ames, and Henry Mancini. Among Webb's greatest hit songs were "Macarthur Park," "By the Time I Get to Phoenix," and "Wichita Lineman."[3]

Up With People, an internationally known up-tempo performing group donned red, white, and blue costumes and exuded optimism about America's future. Lee Allan asked many of his friends to provide lodging for Up With People cast members.

Apollo 10 astronauts Thomas P. Stafford and Eugene A. Cernan were present. The year before, Stafford, a native of Weatherford, Oklahoma, and Cernan flew to within 50,000 feet of the moon's surface in the final mission before American astronauts landed on the moon in the Apollo 11 flight.

It was Lee Allan's idea to not charge admission to the *Stars and Stripes Show*—all anyone had to do was to wear red, white, and blue and be admitted free. On the day of the show, the State Fair Arena was packed to the rafters and a local television audience shared in the patriotic program.

The *Stars and Stripes Show* was a test of Lee Allan's ability to put together a large scale event. James H. Norick, the mayor of Oklahoma City at the time, said, "He passed the test with flying colors! The program was the most successful event ever presented in Oklahoma City!"[4]

Lee Allan had a lot of help in putting together the first *Stars and Stripes Show*. Staff members of Governor Dewey Bartlett, Mayor Norick, and the Oklahoma City Chamber of Commerce helped coordinate events and orchestrated official proclamations and invitations to dignitaries. The show was the climax to "Fly the Flag Month," proclaimed by Governor Bartlett.

The Oklahoma City Association of Broadcasters lent incredible support for the *Stars and Stripes Show*. Lee Allan was president, James Erwin was vice president, and managers of other Oklahoma City broadcast stations served as directors. They included Jacques DeLier, Norman Bagwell, Ben K. West, Tom Reddell, Hewel Jones, Bill Harrison, Ed Thorne, Jerry Lynch, Ron Bonebrake, Omer Thompson, and Ken Hibben.

The cost of the show was underwritten by $250 and $500 individual and business sponsorships sold by Lee Allan. From the beginning, the Oklahoma City Association of Broadcasters intended any profit made from the show be applied to a project to build another of Lee Allan's dreams—a park with a patriotic theme on Lake Hefner.

Early in the planning for the first *Stars and Stripes Show*, Lee Allan looked for land along Lake Hefner to showcase the lake. On his way home from work, he would park along the lake and walk the shore. His car once became stuck in miry clay he had driven into on an abandoned trail. He told a newspaper reporter, "I'd like to see a road running around the edge of the lake, lighted at night. It could be called 'Pride in Oklahoma Drive!'"[5]

In winning official city approval for the park, Lee Allan promised that WKY-Radio and WKY-TV would underwrite

the cost of the project. Special permission was received to display plaques to note contributions of individuals and businesses to build the park. Pat Painter, city planning director, liked Lee Allan's plan and helped push the project through the stages of approval before city commissions and the city council.[6]

At the first *Stars and Stripes Show* were, left to right, songwriter Jimmy Webb, astronaut Tom Stafford, Lee Allan, Governor Dewey Bartlet, Jacque DeLier, and astronaut Gene Cernan, In front is singer Connie Stevens.

The $35,000 in profits from the first show was used to provide equipment and facilities for the Stars and Stripes Park on city-owned land near Wilshire Boulevard and Portland Avenue on the south shore of Lake Hefner. The park, slated to be dedicated in honor of former President and General Dwight D. Eisenhower, included asphalt roads, paddle tennis and volleyball courts, 27 shaded picnic tables, barbecue pits, a 100-seat Bob Hope Picnic Pavilion, playground equipment, and flagpole in a prominent place for the American flag.[7]

One hurdle that had to be overcome before the construction of Stars and Stripes Park could begin was the concern of some city officials that the quality of Lake Hefner would suffer from trash and debris entering the water. However, Mayor Norick guided the project through the planning and zoning commission.

The highlight of the park was Eisenhower Plaza which contained a bust of the late president and flags from the 50 states. Five water jets, symbolizing Eisenhower's five-star general rank, sprayed water into the air from the lake near the plaza.

Before the park was completed a year later, the original estimated cost of $20,000 had grown to $65,000 because a Bob Hope Pavilion and other amenities were added. People

Lee Allan, left, and comedian Red Skelton at the July 4, 1970 dedication of Stars and Stripes Park. President Richard Nixon sent a telegram to Lee Allan to be read at the dedication of the park and the Eisenhower Plaza. Nixon asked Lee Allan to look back to President Eisenhower's first inaugural address in which he spoke of patriotism, moral stamina, and love of liberty. Nixon said, "Your ceremonies in Oklahoma City reflect the fullness of what President Eisenhower was talking about and is the greatest possible tribute to him and his life's enduring work."

were excited about the park and Lee Allan had little dif-
ficulty in convincing citizens to contribute the additional
money to pay for the facility. Companies and groups such as
Kerr-McGee Corporation, TG&Y, the Insurance Association
of Oklahoma City, and Junior Hospitality gave money to
supplement the dollars eventually raised through the *Stars
and Stripes Show*.

In 1970, William C. "Bill" Thrash, program director at Lee
Allan's competitor, KOCO-TV, became director of the *Stars
and Stripes Show* on July Fourth. Thrash, who later worked for

Lee Allan at WKY-TV and became one of the state's foremost television producers and directors at the Oklahoma Educational Television Authority, directed the remaining *Stars and Stripes Shows.*

The 1970 show featured actor Pat Buttram as master of ceremonies with comedian Red Skelton and Anita Bryant as the main performers, and a special appearance by the United States Army Chorus from Fort Myer, Virginia. Apollo 13 Commander James A. Lovell appeared, just months after he and crewmates survived near tragedy in what many called the most epic voyage of survival in the history of man.[8]

A scheduling problem threatened the appearance of Skelton who had been called to the White House to sing for a celebration attended by President Richard Nixon. Lee Allan talked to a presidential assistant about the conflict in scheduling and pointed out how much citizens of Oklahoma were looking forward to being entertained by Skelton. The assistant said, "The president is aware of that, and will make certain Skelton can appear in both places that day."

All Lee Allan was requesting from the White House was that Skelton could be allowed to "get away early." Because the *Stars and Stripes Show* was taped in advance, Lee Allan was able to schedule Skelton's appearance in Oklahoma in time for him to be flown to Washington, D.C. by private jet and the appearance at the White House. The "Skelton-for-Lovell" trade with the White House made everyone happy.[9]

The second show was syndicated to 110 television stations from New York City to Los Angeles and on 100 radio stations, including the Armed Forces Network. Lee Allan was extremely pleased when stations outside the Southwest opted to air the program.[10]

Because of the success of the television program, Bill Thrash and his team spent much of the year working on technical plans to produce the show. Thrash said, "After we rested a day or two after July Fourth, we began mapping out the next year's production. We went into the venue and constructed a stage, curtains, and lights—from the floor up."[11]

The excitement generated by the *Stars and Stripes Show* was noted by state newspapers. *The Daily Oklahoman* editorialized, "We would be at fault if we did not put in a plug for Lee Allan Smith…who conceived the idea for the *Stars and Stripes Show*… Now it focuses favorable national attention on Oklahoma City. We are becoming famous across America for the good work done by Lee Allan."[12]

In 1971, Lee Allan landed a big fish in the entertainment industry—the legendary Bob Hope—for the *Stars and Stripes Show*. Lee Allan was assisted by Hope's publicist, Bill Faith, who suggested that Hope could be attracted to the show through bandleader Les Brown, who had provided music for Hope's shows since 1947. Lee Allan was introduced to Brown by his old Air Force friend Don Klosterman during a golf game at the Bel Air Country Club in Los Angeles. Klosterman later became general manager of the Los Angeles Rams. The string of contacts worked—and Hope agreed to appear on the show.

Hope took Oklahoma by storm. A huge crowd of fans met him at Will Rogers World Airport and followed him as he ate in restaurants and saw the sights of the town. Hope did not seem to mind.

Ever the consummate comedian, Hope said he was surprised by the airport turnout and quipped, "You're not creditors, are you?" The crowd of all ages, from children carried in the parents' arms to barefoot teenagers and grey-haired grandmothers, were watched closely by a dozen plain-clothes police officers, although

it quickly became apparent that the people present wanted to demonstrate for—not against—Hope.[13]

Oklahoma Lieutenant Governor George Nigh and Oklahoma City Mayor Patience Latting officially welcomed Hope to the Sooner State. On meeting the mayor, Hope asked, "You're not part of the women's lib deal are you?" As a gust of wind blew across his face, Hope said, "My hair just went over to Tulsa." Each time Hope had a comment, the crowd cheered. When Hope saw a sign that said, "Welcome Bing," an obvious reference to Hope's longtime friend, Bing Crosby, Hope said, "Bing would be here, but he had an early tee time today."[14]

On Hope's subsequent visits, Lee Allan enlisted the help of Oklahoma City police detective Ken "Sugar" Smith to be Hope's constant companion. Smith knew the city well and could even schedule massages for Hope when he requested them

Lee Allan visits backstage with members of the 1971 *Stars and Stripes Show* cast. Left to right, Miss America Phyllis George, Lee Allan, and singer Kay Starr. Entertainer Jimmy Webb, a frequent guest on the show, said, "Lee Allan always made all the guests feel at home. I was proud to be part of this all-American producton in my home state."

at 1:00 a.m. Smith and Hope became great friends on Hope's next dozen visits to Oklahoma City. Smith and Hope took long walks at night. Smith was Hope's sounding board for jokes—if Smith did not laugh, Hope threw out the joke.[15]

When it came time for the *Stars and Stripes Show*, Lee Allan and Hope bounced ideas off each other and made last minute script changes for master of ceremonies Dale Robertson, an Oklahoma native who continued to live in Oklahoma City, who had been a major box office attraction in films and starred in several television series, including *Wells Fargo.*

Hope charmed the audience with his timeless humor. He said, "This is about the only place left on earth where the impossible dream has a chance of making it. Where but in America can a man like Johnny Cash make a million dollars singing about a railroad that went bankrupt. This really is a land of opportunity. Did you know that 15 years ago, Elvis Presley couldn't spell Tennessee—and now he owns it? What opportunity! Look at Crosby—rich; Sinatra—rich; Dean Martin—loaded."[16]

In addition to Hope and Robertson, the United States Army Band and the United States Army Chorus performed along with The New Christy Minstrels, a popular music singing group; Janos Prohaska, the cookie-mooching bear on the *Andy Williams Show*; and Les Brown and his Band of Renown.[17]

Special guests for the show were Lee Allan's old Air Force friend, Don Klosterman, then general manager of the Baltimore Colts, actor Chill Wills, Oklahoma-born singing sensation Kay Starr, and Miss America Phyllis George.[18]

The 1971 show had a huge sports flavor with appearances by baseball legend Mickey Mantle, Baltimore Colts quarterback Johnny Unitas, and University of Oklahoma football star and Heisman Trophy winner Steve Owens.[19]

As the *Stars and Stripes Show* program expanded, an army of technicians and broadcast staff members were needed. Among those assisting Lee Allan in the major shows of the 1970s were Norm Bagwell, Joe Jerkins, Bill Thrash, J.B. Chase, Doyle Glazier, Gene Lyons, John Bushnell, Greg Robertson, John Spiker, Jay Spivey, Jack Sallaska, Mike Davis, Nick Panos, Marilynn Trimble, Jim Willis, Arne Kattov, Bill Goode, Billie Jean Val'Bracht, Dee Sadler, Danny Williams, and Wakefield Holley.[20]

Bob Hope entertains the sold-out crowd gathered at the State Fair Arena for the taping of the 1971 *Stars and Stripes Show.*

Producing a show with so many entertainers and guests was a challenge for the production team. A unique problem was one with flies left over in the State Fair Arena—attracted to elephants and other animals the week before during the performances of a circus. When Anita Bryant was in the middle of a number, a fly landed right under her nose. However, she kept her composure and finished the song without incident.[21]

After the 1971 show, Bob Hope expressed his desire to

be part of the show every year. He wrote Lee Allan, "I like the idea of your show, and I like the reaction I received from last year's show. I agree with you that it should be an annual affair."[22] Hope had advice for Lee Allan, "Just make sure you get enough

of the celebrities that will appeal to the younger group. They're the ones we really have to sell, because I fear that we've lost a lot of them in the past few years. Try and get the Osmond Brothers, because they're very large with the kids. Also, have NBC work on Flip Wilson. He'd be a big plus."[23]

Lee Allan, creator and executive producer of the *Stars and Stripes Show*, shares a laugh with comedian Bob Hope, left, on a rainy day at the Quail Creek Golf and Country Club. It was a rare event for rain to hamper the Swing for Sight golf tournament. However, Lee Allan turned the rain into a plus for WKY-TV with a live, two-hour show from the country club. Curt Gowdy emceed the show along with Danny Williams and Mary Hart. The rain did not prevent Hope from playing two holes and sharing his unique humor with the live television audience.

In 1972, the NBC Television Network opted to air an hour-long version of the *Stars and Stripes Show* in prime time on July Fourth. NBC wanted to air the program as a network telecast because two-thirds of the 150 television stations across the country that were buying the syndicated show were NBC affiliates. NBC programs were being preempted by the *Stars and Stripes Show*.

The cost of production for the network show for the 240 NBC affiliates was $400,000. To cover the cost, 30-second commercials were sold for $30,000 each. The first two Oklahoma corporations that bought commercials were Phillips Petroleum Company of Bartlesville and Wilson Certified Foods of Oklahoma City.[24]

Other sponsors included the Florida Citrus Commission, Proctor and Gamble, Bufferin, Lipton Tea, McDonald's Restaurants, and the STP Corporation. NBC estimated that 40 million people saw the program—the first time a program of that magnitude had been produced in Oklahoma City for airing on a national television network. Lee Allan was assisted in selling sponsors by Jim Greenwald, his old friend, and head of the Katz Agency in New York City.

The Oklahoma City Chamber of Commerce purchased the last commercial that extolled the benefits of living in Oklahoma City. Leaders such as Dean McGee, Edward Gaylord, Luther Dulaney, and John Kirkpatrick contributed money for the purchase of the final commercial which began with the words, "There's a city that sits in the midst of green trees and blue waters, a city whose people have room enough and reason enough to make it their home."[25]

The actual *Stars and Stripes* program, with Bob Hope as the headliner, was scheduled for taping on July 2, 1972. The masters of ceremonies was Ed McMahon, Johnny Carson's sidekick on *The Tonight Show*. Other featured stars were singers Nancy Wilson, Mickey Newbury, the Johnny Mann Singers, Kenny Rogers, and Les Brown and his Band of Renown, actor Chill Wills, and the Strategic Air Command Band.[26]

Lee Allan had met Rogers backstage at a nightclub in downtown Chicago, Illinois, during an NBC affiliates' meeting. Lee Allan liked Rogers' appeal to younger country and western music fans. When Rogers was given a major slot in the *Stars and Stripes Show*, for only a small talent fee, Hope was perplexed, wondering who Rogers was, and why he was given so much time on the show. In later years, Hope often invited Rogers to appear on his annual specials on NBC.

Sports figures who appeared on the program were Roger Staubach, Johnny Unitas, Steve Owens, Bob Anderson, Mickey Mantle, Don Klosterman, University of Alabama football coach Paul "Bear" Bryant, OU football coach Barry Switzer, Baseball Hall of Fame pitcher Bob Feller, and former OU football coach Bud Wilkinson.[27]

Free tickets for the 1972 show were gone on the first day the box office opened. Even Lee Allan had problems getting extra tickets for friends who decided at the last minute to attend the taping of the show.

During the years of producing the *Stars and Stripes Show*, Bill Thrash worked closely with Lee Allan. Thrash called Lee Allan "an absolute visionary." Thrash said, "He gets an idea, thinks it through, and then puts the team together to make it happen. He knows who to bring on board to carry out his vision."[28]

Bob Hope returned to the *Stars and Stripes Show* stage in 1973. He and Lee Allan had become close friends—Hope

often would telephone Lee Allan in the early hours of the morning to talk about the show—or just life. Once, when Hope appeared at a meeting of 8,000 broadcasters at the National Association of Broadcasters **Lee Allan, right, drinks a cup of coffee while reviewing the *Stars and Stripes* script with master of ceremonies Ed McMahon.**

convention in Las Vegas, Nevada, Hope said, "I'm so glad to be in the same room with so many great broadcasters like Lee Allan Smith of Oklahoma City."[29]

Lee Allan also impressed other stars who came to town. After master of ceremonies Ed McMahon returned to *The Tonight Show*, after appearing on the *Stars and Stripes Show*, host Johnny Carson asked him where he had been. McMahon replied, "I was in Oklahoma City taping the *Stars and Stripes Show*. I was hosted by Lee Allan Smith, impresario of Oklahoma City."[30]

Lee Allan, left, poses with Bill Thrash, center, and Oklahoma Educational Television Authority director Mac Wall, when Thrash was inducted into the Oklahoma Association of Broadcasters Hall of Fame. Thrash was the technical genius who produced most of the *Stars and Stripes Shows.*

When McMahon handed Carson a cowboy hat and a plaque from the Cowboy Hall of Fame in Oklahoma City, Carson poked fun at the museum and appeared bored when he dropped the plaque memorializing Carson's lifetime membership in the Cowboy Hall of Fame on the table.

Carson's actions drew the fire of many Oklahomans. The switchboards at WKY-TV and at NBC in Burbank, California, were busy for almost an hour. *The Daily Oklahoman* printed a sample of letters it received. An Oklahoma City resident wrote, "It reminded me of a spoiled kid who is over indulged with

presents and throws his grandmother's gift on the floor." Other
letter-to-the-editor writers were less offended. A Marietta man
wrote, "Any brilliant comedian will go for a laugh any chance
he gets. Carson got his laugh, and the people of Oklahoma got
their feelings hurt. Carson cuts President Nixon almost every
night."[31]

Carson formally apologized and Lee Allan and Lieutenant
Governor George Nigh encouraged the highly popular talk-
show host to visit the Cowboy Hall of Fame. In a later visit to
Oklahoma City, Lee Allan and Carson, members of the same
fraternity, talked about the two Big Red football teams, OU,
and the University of Nebraska from Carson's home state. In
1985, Lee Allan sent to Carson a football signed by the national
champion OU Sooners.

Lee Allan received encouragement for the patriotic show from
a variety of famous dignitaries. In his files are dozens of tele-
grams from famous citizens such as Reverend Billy Graham and
President Richard Nixon. Graham wrote, "I will be watching on
July 4 with great interest and shall stand up and cheer."[32]

Lee Allan's neighbor, George Short, summed up the success
of the first *Stars and Stripes Show*s, "Lee Allan wanted to do what
he could to bring the American flag, and hence the Stars and
Stripes, back into people's lives. And he did!"[33]

chapter nine

The three girls worship the ground Lee Allan and DeAnn walk on.

—RAY ACKERMAN

FAMILY ON THE MOVE

Lee Allan and DeAnn Smith at their favorite restaurant, Vic 'n Honeys, in Oklahoma City.

L*ee Allan and DeAnn made a joint decision* early in their marriage that she should stay home to take care of their children.

The Smith's history of making joint decisions about the family began with their selection of the name DeLee for their first daughter—it was a combination of their names. The first thing DeLee remembered about her parents was how much they loved each other and liked being together.[1]

As a small child, DeLee sometimes held her breath so long, she would pass out. DeAnn was startled when a pediatrician said, "You better get ready, this little gal is going to have a mind of her own."[2] Fortunately, the holding-the-breath episodes soon ended and DeLee became a delightful child—certainly the most athletic of the three Smith girls.

LEFT: DeLee attended Kanakuk Kamp in Missouri for 15 years as a camper and counselor. In 1977, at age 16, she set the softball throw record.

FAR LEFT: The oldest Smith daughter, DeLee, graduated from Heritage Hall High School in Oklahoma City in 1979. She was the closest to her Dudenhoeffer grand-parents who taught all the girls how to drive in the pasture.

RIGHT: DeLee worked at Harold's, The Webb, and Remington Park.

KAPPA ALPHA THETA
Bid Day - August 21, 1979
University of Oklahoma

DeLee was an all-around
athlete in high school and a member of the Fellowship of Christian
Athletes. Her mother descibes her as a warm person with a very tender
heart. DeLee taught physical education at St. John's Episcopal school.

DeLee attended Belle Isle Elementary School and St. John's Episcopal School through the eighth grade and graduated high school from Heritage Hall in 1979. Four years later, she graduated with a bachelor's degree in family relations and child development from the University of Oklahoma.[3]

Lee Allan was among the busiest fathers in Oklahoma—but his children never knew it. DeLee remembered, "He worked a lot, but we often traveled with him. If he had a broadcasters' convention in a faraway city, he took the whole family."[4]

While at OU, DeLee thought about being a sportscaster. She pledged Kappa Alpha Theta and was heavily involved in intramural sports. Early in life, everyone recognized that DeLee had the electrified energy of her father and the quick smile of her mother.

When DeLee was four years old, DeAnn gave birth to their second daughter, Jennifer, on September 17, 1964. Leigh was intended to be the baby's middle name—but the birth certificate did not reflect DeAnn's instructions, leaving Jennifer officially without a third name.

Lee Allan sang to his girls and helped them say their prayers at bedtime. "He had the most beautiful and melodious voice," Jennifer remembered, "Songs like 'You Are My Sunshine,' 'Scarlet Poppies,' and 'The Sound of Music' put me to sleep immediately. I surely had a smile on my face as I went to sleep with my daddy singing to me."[5]

DeAnn successfully balanced the roles of wife and mother. She was gentle—yet firm. Jennifer said, "She loved completely, with clear vision. She left nothing to chance. You could always read her face. Her varying stages of a smile were the key to her demeanor."[6]

DeAnn was active with her girls in the Mothers Club at Heritage Hall and with her former sorority sisters as a Chi Omega

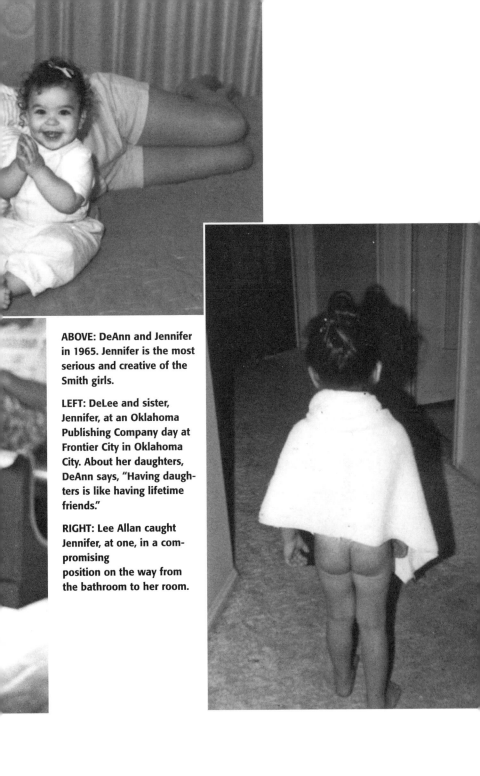

ABOVE: DeAnn and Jennifer in 1965. Jennifer is the most serious and creative of the Smith girls.

LEFT: DeLee and sister, Jennifer, at an Oklahoma Publishing Company day at Frontier City in Oklahoma City. About her daughters, DeAnn says, "Having daughters is like having lifetime friends."

RIGHT: Lee Allan caught Jennifer, at one, in a compromising position on the way from the bathroom to her room.

LEFT: Sixth-grader Jennifer enjoyed wearing her hair braided. She later was named outstanding female junior high student and was football queen at Heritage Hall.

BELOW: Jennifer always had a soft spot in her heart for puppies, indicative of her sweet and caring personality.

alumnus. For several years she volunteered in the Women's Auxiliary at Presbyterian Hospital, taught Vacation Bible School, worked in the school cafeteria at Heritage Hall, and helped in schools wherever her daughters were enrolled. Most of her time, she was "keeping up with the kids," although she always found time to accompany Lee Allan on many business trips.

Jennifer always remembered her parents being together— at preschool and elementary school shows. She attended

Westminster School from preschool to sixth grade, although she also attended kindergarten at Belle Isle Elementary School. In the seventh grade, she switched to Heritage Hall where she graduated in 1982. She was a cheerleader and active in Art Club, Pep Club, chorus, and Fellowship of Christian Athletes at Heritage Hall. She was coached by Molly O'Day in gymnastics and studied modeling with Joanne Fullerton. She received a bachelor's degree in fashion merchandising from the University of Oklahoma in 1986.[7]

After college, Jennifer decided to move to Hollywood to learn film production—even though her father tried to convince her to stay in Oklahoma City. She said, "He did not think that I would like the fast-paced city so far from home." Lee Allan was right—after a few days Jennifer discovered Hollywood was not for her.[8]

She returned to Oklahoma City and worked with her father in preparing for the 1989 Olympic Festival. She worked under the tutelage of Tim O'Toole who later managed the Softball Hall of Fame, the Oklahoma RedHawks, and the State Fair of Oklahoma.

In 1991, Jennifer joined her father at Oklahoma Events, where she remains today. About the same time, Jennifer took the job at Oklahoma Events, DeAnn was diagnosed with cancer. Jennifer and her sisters helped their mother take care of the home during times of exhausting chemotherapy.

"Jennifer was the easiest of the three girls to discipline," said DeAnn. Jennifer would break into tears if either of her parents looked at her sternly—a tendency that has continued into adulthood.

The third Smith daughter, Wendy Blythe Smith, was born April 23, 1974 in Oklahoma City. She attended Westminster

School through the fourth grade and moved to Heritage Hall where she graduated high school in 1992. She was a cheerleader, played tennis, and studied gymnastics under the tutelage of Molly O'Day. In 1996, Wendy graduated

When DeAnn was pregnant with Wendy, DeLee, left, and Jennifer dressed up like their parents in the "with-child" look.

with a bachelor's degree in sociology from the University of Oklahoma. All three Smith sisters were members of the Kappa Alpha Theta sorority at OU.[9]

After college, Wendy worked for Bogo Oil Company, Oklahoma Events, sold commercial real estate and energy information devices, and was a substitute teacher, until she joined her sisters at Oklahoma Events. In 2005, Wendy left Oklahoma

LEFT: Wendy has never met a stranger and is the Smith sister that keeps the family laughing.

RIGHT: Lee Allan and Wendy.

BELOW: Wendy at age 5.

ABOVE: Jennifer, right, and Wendy, wrapping Christmas presents.

Events for a position with Art and Sandy Cotton at Oklahoma City University in events marketing.

Because her sisters were so much older, Wendy really had three mothers. At the time of her birth, DeLee was 13 and Jennifer was 9—a built-in baby-sitting service. Wendy loved the Smith family trips to see California and to Colorado to see family. She so liked the beach, she began calling it "her" ocean. To this day, when the family heads for a beachside resort, Lee Allan says, "Let's go to Wendy's ocean!"[10]

Lee Allan was stricter with the two older girls than with Wendy. "He trusted us," said Wendy, "but was far more lax with me." In high school, with a twinkle in her eye, Wendy asked her father if she could extend her nightly curfew by 30 minutes. Lee Allan softly said, "Okay."[11]

Lee Allan and DeAnn were consistent parents—they talked about decisions for the girls and presented a united front. Neither was susceptible to many childrens' antics of not liking an answer from

RIGHT: Oilman Dean McGee presents Lee Allan with the silver medal award of the Advertising Federation.

one parent and asking the same question of the other parent—hoping for a different decision. If the girls disobeyed and played with the moss and frogs in the creek on the golf course across the street from their home, they often saw their mother

standing in the front yard with a yardstick in her hand, although she never used it.[12]

DeAnn called her daughters home with a dinner bell Lee Allan installed. The bell could be heard in playmates' yards for two blocks. The girls knew they were needed immediately and dared not delay their return.

DeAnn was a superb cook. She was famous for her spaghetti because that is what DeLee and Lee Allan frequently requested for dinner. DeLee said, "She makes spaghetti different than anyone else on earth!"[13] DeAnn was never afraid to try a

The Smith girls in 2003. Left to right, Wendy, Jennifer, and DeLee.

new recipe—and usually they liked it. Dinner was a family affair. If guests were present, DeAnn tried to make them feel special.

Lee Allan was always protective of his girls. Even after they graduated from college and lived at home, they had curfews. If Wendy was out later than usual, Lee Allan would call her the next day and ask where she was. His subtle comment was often, "Isn't that a little late for a single girl to stay out?"[14]

Each of the Smith girls is different. Collectively, they agree that DeLee was independent, Jennifer was innocent, and Wendy was mischievous. An example was when Jennifer was preparing for her 2002 marriage to George "Fritz" Kiersch. While shopping for a dress to wear to the rehearsal dinner, Wendy convinced Jennifer to buy a certain dress. Wendy, who wanted to wear the dress herself, said, "I love this outfit! This would look great on you!" Wendy talked Jennifer into the buying the dress—and then she wore it.[15]

DeAnn provides interesting descriptions of her three daughters—DeLee and her father are close because of their love for sports—Jennifer is "very particular" and soft-spoken—Wendy is a combination of both of her older sisters, but sometimes "a little prissy!"[16]

In addition to spending a lot of time in his oasis at home, Lee Allan loves his neighbors—and they love him. The Smiths and George and Margaret Short have been neighbors for more than 40 years. George Short said, "Lee Allan is much more than a neighbor, he is a friend. I can talk over my problems with him—and know he will listen and take time to share his thoughts with me."[17]

Lee Allan's famous good nature is not just displayed in public, but in private situations. In the mid 1970s, Silkey Wilson began a lawn service and was hired to maintain the lawn for Lee Allan's neighbor across the street. As Wilson and his son, Mark, pulled away from the curb one day, the utility trailer that carried their lawn maintenance equipment unavoidably ran over Jennifer's dog. A neighbor summoned Lee Allan who took the dog into his arms, loaded the animal into his Lincoln, and headed for the veterinarian's office.[18]

The next week, Wilson was mowing the lawn across the street when he saw Lee Allan approaching. Wilson thought, "Oh No!, I'm really in trouble now!" However, Lee Allan said, "Are you the nice man who ran over my dog?" Wilson answered affirmatively and Lee Allan promptly hired him to maintain his lawn, a relationship that continued in 2005.[19]

Lee Allan and DeAnn always had close contact with their extended families. He was a favorite of their nieces and nephews, who loved to visit "Uncle Lee and Aunt DeAnn." Ann Smith, the wife of Lee Allan's brother, Dale, said, "Lee Allan always treated me like a sister. He always surprised us at Christmas with the most innovative and fun gifts. He had to spend hours trying to figure out what to give."[20]

Once, Lee Allan decided to give his brother a miniature model of Dale and Ann's rustic cabin located in Green Mountain Falls, Colorado. After the model was made, Lee Allan was hesitant about shipping it to Colorado. Instead, he went to Will Rogers World Airport in Oklahoma City and paid a soldier who was flying to Denver to hand carry the model to Dale. On another occasion, Lee Allan sent a bucket of Dale's favorite ice cream, Kaiser's, via a stranger flying from Oklahoma City to Denver. On other occasions, Lee Allan sent a case of barbecue sauce from Dale's favorite, Han's Barbecue in Oklahoma City.[21]

LEFT: Dale, Lee Allan's brother, and his wife, Ann.

BELOW: Left to right, Charley, Carl, Nadie, Carl Jr., Walter, and Clay Smith.

During Dale's illness before his death, Lee Allan would often fly to Colorado to spend time with him. Lee Allan went out of the way to take Dale to the Ed Podalak-Jimmy Buffet Golf Tournament in Aspen, Colorado, during a very difficult period of Dale's final illness. There they met Lee Allan's longtime friend, Podolak, a former Kansas City Chiefs professional football star.[22]

ABOVE: Lee Allan's brother, Donald, and his wife, Betty Lou.

Dale and Ann's children, Shane, Drew, and Elizabeth, thought Uncle Lee was the most fun person in the world. They enjoyed attending the *Stars and Stripes Shows* and meeting the famous personalities in town for the event. Even as an adult, Elizabeth Smith Brunsdon, who considers Lee Allan "a second dad," and her family are often met with welcome posters when they arrive at the Smith home in Oklahoma City for a visit.[23]

"Our families do a lot of laughing together!" Elizabeth remembered, "Something is always going on. Keeping up with three girls at home can be tricky for Uncle Lee, but he just laughs at the craziness, although he does sneak away for an occasional nap." When Elizabeth and her cousins were younger, they often walked around the house carrying pillows, so as not to awake Lee Allan. Elizabeth said, "We laughed so hard, we had to muffle the sound!"[24]

LEFT: Lee Allan feeds DeAnn a taste of his birthday cake.

RIGHT: Drew Smith, Lee Allan's nephew, and his wife, Jean, and daughter, Gemma.

LEFT: The family of Lee Allan's nephew, Vernon, who lives in Arlington, Texas. Left to right, Chap, Vernon, Lynda, and Bryan.

RIGHT: Shane Smith and family live in Cheyenne, Wyoming. Left to right, Rio, Shane, Aiden, and Paige.

RIGHT: Donald, left, and daughter, Dana Smith Gooley. Her three daughters are Sherry, Michelle, and Jennifer Gooley.

BELOW: Lee Allan and niece, Elizabeth Smith Brunsdon. After the death of her father, Dale, "Uncle Lee" filled a huge void in her life.

RIGHT: Elizabeth Brunsdon, Lee Allan's niece, and her children, Daniel, and Elizabeth, pose at the Oklahoma City Zoo with Wendy and Jennifer.

RIGHT: Jennifer Smith married George "Fritz" Kiersch on September 21, 2002.

BELOW: Lee Allan and DeAnn treasure friendships. Left to right, Bob Robinson, Ed de Cordova, Beth Ann Sadler, Nancy de Cordova, and Dee Sadler.

BELOW: Left to right, Carson, Caroline, Carl Jr., and Carol Smith.

chapter ten

Lee Allan took a dream and made the Stars and Stripes Show *the most exciting event in Oklahoma City.*

—JIM GREENWALD

A PROMOTER'S PROMOTER

DeAnn, left, and songwriter Burt Bacharach at an Oklahoma City concert.

T he success of the **Stars and Stripes Show** gained Lee Allan a reputation as a superb promoter of Oklahoma values and attractions. He was executive producer of the fifth annual *Stars and Stripes Show* in 1973. He was ably assisted by producer Dick Schneider, associate producer Joe Jerkins, and director Bill Thrash. Barry Downs was the chief writer for the show which featured Tennessee Ernie Ford as the master of ceremonies.[1]

The musical guests were Doc Severinsen, musical director of *The Tonight Show*; Today's Children, an energetic young singing group; Lou Rawls; Anita Bryant; and Les Brown and his Band of Renown. Celebrities

Tennessee Ernie Ford, the "old pea picker himself," at a special dinner at the Smith home before the 1973 *Stars and Stripes Show.* A culinary highlight of the dinner was Ford cooking his own special cornbread recipe, which Lee Allan called the "best cornbread" he had ever eaten. Left to right, Elizabeth Smith, Ann Smith, Jennifer Smith and DeAnn Smith.

who appeared at the July 1 taping at the Myriad Convention Center in downtown Oklahoma City included Oklahoma-born Colonel Robinson Risner, the highest ranking American prisoner of war in the Vietnam War; Mickey Mantle; Steve Owens; Detroit Lions quarterback Greg Landry; Grambling University coach Eddie Robinson; Los Angeles Lakers basketball star Happy Hairston; Oklahoma Olympic gold medal winner Wayne Wells; former OU coach Bud Wilkinson; and astronaut Alan B. Shepard, Jr.

NBC broadcast the taped one-hour show in its prime spot, 10:00 p.m. Eastern Standard Time. Bob Hope led the entire cast in singing the finale, "America the Beautiful."[2]

It took a lot of people to put on the *Stars and Stripes Show.* Lee Allan tabbed many of his friends such as George and Margaret

Short, Dee and Beth Ann Sadler, Ed and Nancy de Cordova, Ron and Florence Richey, and Mick and Jeannette Evenson to host celebrities. The wives of some of the athletes were taken on shopping trips while their husbands rehearsed or played golf.

Other friends were put to work lining up limousines, arranging for flowers, and making hotel accommodations for guests. Cathy Hutton, later Kirk, was Lee Allan's executive assistant and saw how intense he operated during the weeks before the annual show. Lee Allan kept a notepad by his nightstand so he could write down ideas when they kept him from sleeping. He also asked Kirk to keep a pad and pencil by her bed so she would not forget a random detail that went through her mind at night. "He taught me that nothing was impossible," Kirk remembered.[3]

Kirk believes one of the secrets of the success of the *Stars and Stripes Show*s was Lee Allan's invitation to performers' families to attend the event. It cost more money for airfare and hotel rooms for families, but spouses and children of entertainers fell in love with Oklahoma City, and encouraged the entertainers to return the following year.

Ed McMahon once brought his young son for whom Lee Allan wanted to provide a memorable welcome to Oklahoma City. Lee Allan arranged for cowboys on horseback from the Frontier City Amusement Park to overtake the automobile in which the McMahons were riding. Young McMahon was presented with a cowboy hat and boots. For weeks after the trip, the boy told everyone how he had been held up in a stage coach robbery.[4]

Lee Allan thought of last minute details that would make stars want to be part of the *Stars and Stripes Show*. One year, he asked Kirk to find out which were Dionne Warwick's favorite chocolates. When Kirk discovered that the singer loved Russell Stover candies, she was dispatched to Warwick's hotel room with a box of the finest candies to be placed on her nightstand. Later Warwick was presented with a fine Steuben crystal dolphin.

Lee Allan also made sure Bob Hope had plenty of fresh orange juice and lemon pie in his dressing room. Hope stayed in private homes arranged by Lee Allan. On separate occasions Bud Bouse and Jack and Judy Hodges hosted Hope in their homes.[5]

Once Hope arrived at the last minute and had forgotten his jokes written by his staff in California. Kirk took shorthand and transcribed the jokes while they were read by Hope's writers on the telephone.

In 1974, Bob Hope, Tennessee Ernie Ford, and Miss America Rebecca Ann King welcomed many returning guests and newcomers—OU football stars Billy Vessels and Greg Pruitt, the Texas Boys Choir, football heroes "Mean" Joe Greene and Craig Morton, dancer Juliet Prowse, and singer John Davidson.[6]

In 1975, local television personality Gaylon Stacey warmed up the live audience at the Myriad before master of ceremonies John Davidson, who stayed in Tom Dulaney's home, took over the program. Country music

Lee Allan, right, welcomes actor Telly Savalis to Oklahoma City and the *Stars and Stripes Show*.

star Charley Pride and the Mike Curb Congregation provided musical numbers, backed up by Les Brown's band, Anita Bryant, Juliet Prowse, and Bob Hope, who publicly declared Oklahoma City was his favorite annual trip outside California.[7]

The Stars and Stripes Chorale, a group of local musicians, directed by John Blackwell, provided the musical backdrop for big name entertainers. Ann Vinson, writing in *The Daily Oklahoman,* called the seventh annual show, "a rousing evening of pure entertainment." Vinson wrote, "Move over motherhood and apple pie. Make room in the Americanism picture for the *Stars and Stripes Show.*" [8]

The annual budget for the show ballooned and Lee Allan had to make the decision to begin charging admission to the annual event.

The charge did not deter huge crowds of 13,000 people packing the Myriad. The audience at the taping of the show even enjoyed mistakes. When scenes or songs had to be re-taped, the audience looked on in wonder. Oklahoma City residents who were fortunate enough to obtain tickets marveled at Hope delivering his rapid-fire, deadpan humor. Every word of the monologue was printed in bold, black letters on cue cards elevated on a platform in front

Lee Allan presents legendary singer Kate Smith with a Steuben crystal bird after rehearsal for the Bicentennial *Stars and Stripes Show*. At the microphone is Tennessee Ernie Ford.

of him at center stage. Two men turned and stacked the oversized cards and somehow kept up with his polished delivery.[9]

Jim Greenwald, Lee Allan's longtime friend, had become president of the Katz Agency in New York City. After watching the 1975 show, Greenwald wrote Lee Allan, "You did it again! P.T. Barnum has nothing on you. Yours was truly a Herculean effort…In seven years you have taken a dream and made it into the most exciting event in Oklahoma City."[10]

"Happy 200th Birthday" was the theme of the eighth annual presentation of the *Stars and Stripes Show* in 1976, the year of America's Bicentennial celebration. The show was taped earlier than usual for a June 30th two-hour national prime time telecast on NBC. The show was still the only network television show produced by a local television station.

The 1976 show was one of the spectacular patriotic television programs ever produced. Milton DeLugg was musical director and Jim Bates choreographed dance and musical numbers. Returning for a third time as master of ceremonies was Tennessee Ernie Ford. Also returning were astronauts Eugene Cernan and Alan Shepard, Anita Bryant, Ed McMahon, and Dionne Warwick who sang a medley of her popular music hits. Because of contractual obligations to do his own Bicentennial show, Bob Hope was unable to be part of the 1976 program. Hope and Lee Allan later laughed together because the *Stars and Stripes Show* drew better ratings than did Hope's special.[11]

Newcomers for the Bicentennial show were Kate Smith, best remembered for her rendition of "God Bless America," comedian Frank Gorshin, the Fifth Dimension, Broadway star Chita Rivera, the Young Americans, General Daniel "Chappie" James, Jr., commander in chief of the North American Defense Command, and Mike Douglas, who began his television career at WKY-TV.

Smith's singing of "God Bless America" left the audience standing and cheering. It was the last time Smith performed the song in a concert before her death.

Sports celebrities such as Mickey Mantle, Steve Owens, Billy Vessels, Ralph Neely, Barry Switzer, Gale Sayers, Johnny Unitas, George Blanda, Steve Bartkowski, Whitey Ford, Joe Greene, and Rocky Bleier, played in the annual Stars and Stripes Golf Tournament, in addition to appearing on the program. Money raised in the golf tournament helped buy equipment for a radio station on the campus of Langston University.[12]

E.K. Gaylord Boulevard in downtown Oklahoma City was turned into a mini-Hollywood for the taping of segments for the show. Ed McMahon led a smiling female entourage of Miss America, Miss Black America, Miss Rodeo America, the Ada, Oklahoma, High School marchers called The Couganns, and the 55-piece Strategic Air Command Band down the street, mimicking the huge welcome he received on his arrival in Oklahoma City.[13]

For his work on the Bicentennial *Stars and Stripes Show*, Lee Allan was given the Abraham Lincoln Bicentennial Award from the Southern Baptist Convention. President Gerald Ford sent a congratulatory telegram to Lee Allan for the occasion. The Oklahoma Broadcasters Association honored Lee Allan with a special award and commissioned Doyle Glazier, art director of WKY-TV, to paint a portrait of Lee Allan. Glazier also had served as art director for the *Stars and Stripes Shows*.

Lee Allan also won three Freedom Foundation George Washington honor medals, and medals of honor from the Daughters of the American Revolution, the American Legion, and the Veterans of Foreign Wars.

Lee Allan had nursed the *Stars and Stripes Show* from a performance by a handful of celebrities to an unprecedented array

of personalities from entertainment, government, military, and sports. However, Lee Allan recommended to the board of directors of the Oklahoma City Association of Broadcasters that the Bicentennial show be the last. In announcing the cessation of the eight-year run of the show, Lee Allan said, "If one child is now able to hold up his head with pride in the heritage of the United States of America, and what our country stands for, it's been well worth all the time, money, and effort."[14]

DeAnn and Lee Allan pose with the portrait of Lee Allan by Doyle Glazier. The portrait was commissioned by the Oklahoma Broadcasters Association to honor Lee Allan for his work producing the *Stars and Stripes Show* and promoting the construction of Stars and Stripes Park. Unfortunately, the portrait disappeared and has never been found.

A year after the last show, associate producer Joe Jerkins wrote Lee Allan, "I miss the hustle and the intense creative activity. But most of all, I miss the close association with you. Few, if any, know how intensely you devoted yourself to the project, how many sleepless nights you had, or how much the success of the project depended on you and you alone. Without your dedication, and worry, and sweat, there would have been no show, or park."[15]

Lee Allan's friends sometimes benefited from meeting so many celebrities in connection the *Stars and Stripes Show*s. Advertising executive Jim Greenwald had met Mickey Mantle playing in the Stars and Stripes Golf Tournament. Later, in New York City, Greenwald sat beside Mantle at a restaurant at the Regency Hotel and said, "Lee Allan Smith says to tell you hello." Mantle had a blank stare, but agreed to sign a baseball for the son of a friend of Greenwald. After the Yankee superstar signed the baseball, he looked at Greenwald and said, "I'm doing this for Lee Allan!"[16]

Despite all the hoopla surrounding the *Stars and Stripes Show*, Lee Allan had helped lead WKY-Radio and WKY-TV to a super success-

Lee Allan hired young Oklahoma baseball players to provide analysis for WKY-TV during the World Series. Left to right, Bobby Murcer, a New York Yankees star from Oklahoma City, Lee Allan, and Johnny Bench, a Cincinnati Reds star from Binger, Oklahoma.

ful decade. He had a huge role in convincing Bob Barry to become the fulltime sports director of WKY-TV, to replace Mike Treps.

Lee Allan, Bill Morgan, owner of KNOR Radio in Norman, and Jim Bellatti of Stillwater, were the prime movers of Network Services, an entity that owned the broadcast rights to OU football and basketball games. When Network Services lost the bid to continue the broadcasts, Lee Allan went to bat for Barry with Edward L. Gaylord who allowed Barry to broadcast OU games even though WKY-Radio's competitor, KTOK, had won the contractual rights. To make the transition work, Barry was actually fired at WKY-TV and rehired on a contract basis. In 1972, Barry began an 18-year stint broadcasting the Oklahoma State University football games, although he continued as sports director at Channel Four. He later returned to the microphone as the OU play-by-play announcer.[17]

In 1974, OU was 11-0 under Coach Barry Switzer, but could not attend a bowl game because of probation imposed by the National Collegiate Athletic Association (NCAA). To give Sooner fans something to cheer about in the bowl season, Lee Allan dreamed up a mythical bowl game between OU and Notre Dame University.[18]

For three weeks, Barry and his longtime color analyst on OU broadcasts, Jack Ogle, also a news anchor at Channel Four, scripted a game and taped the play-by-play. Lee Allan was able to get ABC sportscaster Howard Cosell to be the halftime guest of the dream game. The Cosell interview was by telephone so Barry and Ogle had to come up with some idea to explain why his voice sounded like it was on the telephone. During the interview, Barry said, "We're on the west side of the stadium and Howard Cosell is on the east side, so we are going to do the interview by phone."[19]

The 1974 dream bowl game ended right for Sooner fans when defensive standout Lucious Selmon intercepted a Notre Dame pass and scored a go-ahead touchdown. When Notre Dame went ahead, the script called for Grant Burget to score the winning touchdown for OU. The dream game was such a hit, the Oklahoma legislature passed a resolution commending the project.[20]

In 1976, WKY-TV was sold by the Gaylord family because of a proposed Federal Communications Commission rule that limited ownership of radio and television stations and newspapers in a single market. The new owner was The Evening News Association, the company that published the *Detroit Evening News*. The call letters of the station were changed to KTVY. Lee Allan moved from his dual role as assistant manager of both radio and television stations to vice president of Gaylord Broadcasting Company and general manager of WKY-Radio.

No one in Oklahoma City was more active in civic affairs. Lee Allan served as president, chairman, or director of Allied Arts, the Oklahoma City Zoological Society, Better Business Bureau, Oklahoma City Chamber of Commerce, Junior Achievement, Young Mens Christian Association (YMCA), Oklahoma Choral Association, Oklahoma City All Sports Association, Oklahoma Medical Research Foundation, Oklahoma Safety Council, Oklahoma Symphony Orchestra, Heritage Hall School, United Way, Boy Scouts, Goodwill Industries, and Girl Scouts. If a program benefited Oklahoma City, Lee Allan was interested and threw his full support—time and money-raising skills—behind the effort.

Lee Allan assisted in a fund raising drive that raised $31 million to assure the construction of Presbyterian Medical Center. He also actively promoted the selection of Oklahoma City as the site for the American Bowling Congress tournament in 1976. Lee Allan created so much good publicity for the Oklahoma City Zoo that zoo officials named a newly-born hippopotamus for him. A newspaper story pointed out that the animal was named for Lee Allan for his contributions to the zoo, and "not because of any physical attributes."[21]

Also for the zoo, Lee Allan persuaded his friend Bob Hoover to provide funds necessary to buy a paddle-wheel steamboat that was named Virginia, in honor of Hoover's daughter.

In 1975, Lee Allan began helping The Society to Prevent Blindness in Oklahoma (PBO) raise money for an annual Swing for Sight golf tournament. The tournament was organized and supported by OU football coach Barry Switzer and former OU coach Bud Wilkinson. Lee Allan moved the tournament to Quail Creek Golf and Country Club and, with the leadership of executive director, Martha Pat Upp, made the annual tournament a huge success. Lee Allan was able to bring Mickey Mantle, Don Cherry, Bob Hope, Barbara Eden, Dinah Shore, and other sports and entertainment personalities to play in the "Dream of Dreams" tournament sponsored by individuals and businesses who contributed up to $500 per person for the right to play with the celebrities.[22]

"Lee Allan had the power and ability for recruiting not only celebrities, but also many golfers," Upp said. At times, however, it was a little scary for Upp because she had no idea what methods Lee Allan would use to impress players in the tournament. One night during a banquet, she looked up and saw people wearing Indian costumes coming into the room—Lee Allan's extra touch in presenting a feather headdress to an entertainer. When Ed McMahon was honored, he was given a special name in the Otoe Indian language, a word that meant "big voice."[23]

At one Swing for Sight tournament, OU football rookie Joe Washington was playing golf for the first time. He arrived at the country club with his huge, black football cleats on. He remembered, "Like a father, Lee Allan came to my car and said, 'Son, just

RIGHT: Lee Allan brought football legend Johnny Unitas, left, to many Oklahoma City charity events. Unitas said, "The best thing you can say about Lee Allan is that he's my friend, because in life, you don't have very many friends, you have a lot of acquaintances." Unitas was one of the few celebrities with whom Lee Allan would dine after a show. On Unitas' last trip to Oklahoma City, Lee Allan took him and his wife, Sandy, to see the Oklahoma City National Memorial. After Unitas' death, Sandy, said, "Lee Allan always made us feel at home in Oklahoma City. He was patient and took care of every detail to make our visit pleasurable."

BELOW: There was always a lot of laughing during the Swing for Sight golf tournament. Left to right, oil man Bill Saxon, attorney Jimmy Linn, Lee Allan, actor James Garner, and Danny Williams. Linn was nominated for most valuable player of the group, but the motion died for lack of a second. When Lee Allan nominated Garner for induction into the Oklahoma Hall of Fame, Garner wrote, "This is the highest honor I could receive—and could not have achieved it without your help! For a country boy from Norman to be honored in this way is truly far above anything I could ever have dreamed of!"

RIGHT: Lee Allan assisted Vinita Cravens to bring actress Carol Channing, right, to Oklahoma City in 1977 to star in the stage production of *Hello Dolly.* After the performance, she sent a telegram to Lee Allan, "I know you liked the new show because I saw you and Barry Switzer right down front on opening night...Lee Allan, you are a better arranger than me."

put your tennis shoes on, and that'll be Okay!'" Washington had only been told to be at the country club at a certain time "with his cleats on!" That incident led to a father-son relationship between Lee Allan and "Little Joe" who went on from record-breaking seasons for the Sooners to a stellar career in professional football.[24]

Lee Allan's efforts to raise money for charitable and civic causes in the 1970s were widely applauded. University of Oklahoma President Bill Banowsky said, "He is one of those unselfish servants about which the Bible speaks, 'He who would be greatest among you must become the servant of all.'"[25] Fred Zahn said, "He was extremely capable of recruiting people and getting them to do a job that needed to be done. People just followed his lead."[26] Oklahoma City Mayor James Norick received so many calls from Lee Allan on so many different projects, he often thought, "What is it this time?"[27]

Once when a newspaper reporter asked Lee Allan how he could pull off yet another spectacular project, Lee Allan showed him a gold-colored coin he had carried since his Air Force days. Emblazoned on the coin were the words, "Negative thoughts bring negative results." The other side of the coin read, "Anything the mind of man can conceive, he can achieve." Lee Allan told the reporter, "Part of what I do is for my own satisfaction, and certainly for my family. But it's more than that. You couldn't blast me out of this city. I love it. That's the main thing that started me, and that's the thing that keeps me going now."[28]

Lee Allan did not stay away from television station management long. In 1978, Norman Bagwell, general manager of KTVY-TV died, and Lee Allan was selected to replace him. The new manager of WKY-Radio was Lee Allan's longtime friend, Dee Sadler.

To promote the revival of the musical, *Oklahoma!,* Lee Allan had a surrey with fringe on top built and transported to Hollywood for the opening. The surrey was prominently displayed in front of the

Pantages Theater for the opening. While in California, the surrey was taken to the home of Tulsa native Shirley Jones who had played in the original movie, *Oklahoma!*. While interviewing Jones about her role in the movie, KTVY's Mary Hart so impressed Jones' husband, Marty Ingles, that he became her manager for a short time.

At the time, Hart appeared each day in Oklahoma City alongside Danny Williams on KTVY's popular variety show, *Dannysday*, but she was interested in hosting a national show. Lee Allan believed Hart would be excellent for national television but asked her to promise that if she ever returned to Oklahoma City, she would return to Channel Four. Hart agreed, hired an agent, and soon became co-host of *P.M. Magazine* in Los Angeles. Later she became a national star on *Entertainment Tonight*.

Hart called her friend, Kerry Robertson, who lived in Hollywood. Robertson wanted to return to her hometown of Oklahoma City, so she auditioned for, and won the job as Williams' co-host on *Dannysday*. KTVY-TV program director Bill Thrash called Robertson to tell her she had beaten out 134 other applicants for the spot on the local show. Robertson and Hart literally changed apartments—Hart went to Hollywood and Robertson came home to Oklahoma City.[29]

The surrey followed the opening of *Oklahoma!* to Washington, D.C., and to Broadway in New York City. In the nation's capital, a wheel on the surrey broke. Fortunately, a new wheel was shipped from craftsmen in a Mennonite community Pennsylvania in time for the surrey's appearance. Another tense moment for the Oklahoma delegation arose when Vinita Cravens' husband, Del, suffered a heart attack.

The surrey also appeared outside the Civic Center Music Hall when *Oklahoma!* played in Oklahoma City, a production that was due largely to the efforts of Vinita Cravens. Lee Allan's promotional efforts using the surrey resulted in huge publicity for the musical

Whatever the project, Lee Allan simply has Oklahoma City at heart. Nothing he has done has been for personal gain.

—TOM McDANIEL

He is a very rare breed. There are only a few people in America who have the ability to do the things he does.

—JOHNNY UNITAS

CHAMPION FUND RAISER

Lee Allan was an avid supporter of the Oklahoma City Zoo. In this publicity photograph, he had a orangutan clinging to his back. Lee Allan's love for the zoo began in childhood with a popular polar bear named Carmichael and Monkey Island.

O*klahomans have long stood in awe* of Lee Allan's ability to raise huge sums of money for worthwhile projects. During the many years as a broadcasting executive, he gave thousands of hours of his personal time to promote good causes. He was not at all bashful about asking individuals and businesses for money and in-kind contributions. Sugar Smith said, "If he had a minimum wage for his volunteer hours for this city and threw it into a pot, the pot would be worth several million dollars."[1]

Almost every major civic project in Oklahoma City in the last third of the 20th century was covered with Lee Allan's fingerprints. Devon Energy Chairman Larry Nichols said, "One cannot drive many miles in the Oklahoma City metropolitan area without passing some facility or program that Lee Allan has benefited."[2] Auto dealer Jackie Cooper said, "All Oklahomans owe him a big thank you for making Oklahoma a state you are proud to be from."[3]

Philanthropist Jose Freede says that Lee Allan knows more people than anyone else in Oklahoma.[4] Lee Allan's neighbor, George Short, has a lasting wish, "Someday, when I'm with him, I'm going to run into a person, a stranger, who does not know him—then I'll get to introduce Lee Allan as my neighbor."[5]

Lee Allan had a full-time job as general manager of Channel Four in the 1980s. However, it was his promotion of a variety of projects for which he was best known. He was an officer or member of the boards of almost every Oklahoma City civic organization. Hardly a week passed without local news coverage of Lee Allan being appointed to another board, heading the United Way drive, raising money for Allied Arts, helping Boy Scouts, or chairing a $2.5 million fund-raising campaign for Oklahoma Christian College.

In 1982, he was executive producer of the Diamond Jubilee Show, the finale to Oklahoma's 75th birthday celebration. By using his star-studded Rolodex, Lee Allan was able to bring Oklahoma-born stars such as James Garner and Patti Page home for the evening of entertainment at Oklahoma City's Myriad Convention Center. In addition to Garner and Page, jazz guitarist Barney Kessel, comedian Argus Hamilton, and band leader Harry James, originally from Ada, Oklahoma, appeared.[6]

Others returning to the state for the celebration included Will Rogers, Jr.; Candice Early, star of the soap opera, *All My Children*; singers Sammi Smith, Jimmy Webb, Henson Cargill, and Jody Miller; CBS newsman Douglas Edwards; baseball star Mickey Mantle; football coach Barry Switzer; track star J.W. Mashburn; sportscaster Ross Porter; former Miss America Jane Jayroe; actress Rue McClanahan; and actor Ben Johnson.[7]

Lee Allan was assisted in the Diamond Jubilee finale production by Bill Thrash and Carveth Osterhaus. The musical director was Joel Levine, associate conductor of the Oklahoma Symphony Orchestra. After the program, Diamond Jubilee Commission chairman Jack T. Conn told Lee Allan, "It was superb. I was elated over the whole show and was ecstatic about the size of the audience."[8]

In 1982, Lee Allan became chairman of a special project to build an elaborate aquarium project, dubbed "Aquaticus," at the Oklahoma City Zoo, the oldest zoo in the Southwest. In announcing a $1 million gift from The Noble Foundation to kick off the campaign, Lee Allan said, "We're on the five-yard line, but we need the support of all Oklahomans."[9]

By the following year, Lee Allan and his team of helpers had raised more than $4.5 million to build Aquaticus. Groundbreaking was held on October 1, 1983, and the 65,000-square-feet marine life facility opened one year later. At the time, it contained the most comprehensive collection of aquatic life in the central region of the United States. The facility had a huge amphitheater for dolphin shows, a laboratory, and a naturalistic exhibition area.[10]

For his work on the Aquaticus project and his service to the Oklahoma Zoological Society, Lee Allan was honored at a black-tie event. He also was named civic leader of the year and marketer of the year by the Sales & Marketing Executives Association and received one of the first H.H. Herbert Distinguished Alumni Awards from the University of Oklahoma School of Journalism.

ABOVE: Comedian Tim Conway pokes fun at Lee Allan during a luncheon honoring contributors to Festival of the Horse.

BELOW: Lee Allan, ever a strong supporter of University of Oklahoma athletics, talks to future OU and professional football superstars in 1984. Left to right, Keith Jackson, Lee Allan, and Troy Aikman.

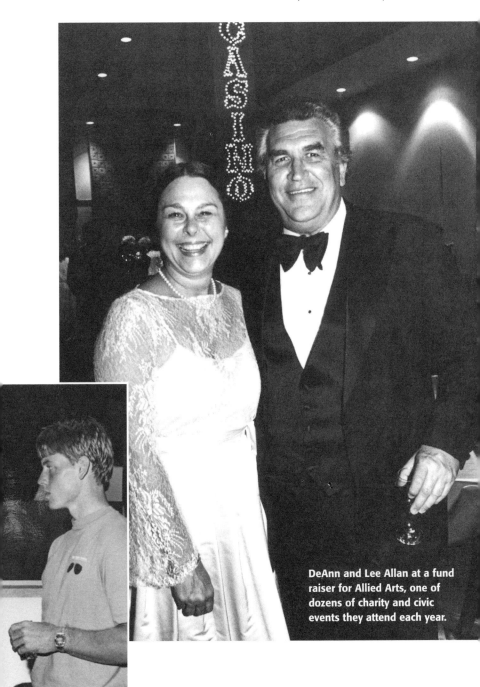

DeAnn and Lee Allan at a fund raiser for Allied Arts, one of dozens of charity and civic events they attend each year.

In the 1980s, he was also presented the Silver Medal Award from the Oklahoma City Advertising Club, named Oklahoman of the Year by the Oklahoma Association of Broadcasters, and was given the Humanitarian Award by the Oklahoma City Public School Foundation. At the dinner honoring him for the school foundation award, Oklahoma City Mayor Andy Coats called Lee Allan, "Mr. Oklahoma City." Publisher Edward L. Gaylord said, "Lee Allan spends 100 percent of his time loving Oklahoma City."[11]

In 1985, Lee Allan began a three-year stint as chairman of the Oklahoma City Chamber of Commerce, a highly visible position that lends itself to the elite of leadership in Oklahoma's capital city. When a hitch developed in any city project, Lee Allan got the call. For example, when funding for the Crystal Bridge seemed to be in limbo, oil man Dean McGee called on Lee Allan to save the project.

Lee Allan used the chamber chairman post to challenge Oklahoma City residents to dream about the future. He suggested an ambitious venture that would repair the city's infrastructure, renovate downtown, attract a major league sports team, and make Oklahoma City a prime mover in the highly-competitive convention business. As the population of the metropolitan area neared one million, Lee Allan told chamber members the key to growth was being positive.

He chaired community-wide meetings to seek input on establishing goals. When the comments of citizens and leaders were tallied, economic development was given top priority. Lee Allan was proud to report a 4,000 net job increase in the Oklahoma City job market during his first year as leader of the chamber of commerce.[12]

After Oklahoma City's loss of the National Finals Rodeo, Lee Allan and the chamber board began a new program calculated to lure horse shows to the State Fairgrounds Arena. Within a short time, Oklahoma City had more horse shows than any other city.

As a break from the serious business of promoting Oklahoma City, Lee Allan participated in a lively tribute to publisher Edward L. Gaylord and his wife, Thelma, in September, 1985. Lee Allan, Mayor Andy Coats, Oklahoma Christian College President Dr. Terry Johnson, and publisher Leland Gourley performed a series of skits based on the television program *Hee Haw*, produced by Gaylord's company that owned the Grand Old Opry and the Opryland Entertainment Complex in Nashville, Tennessee.[13]

"This has not been a Gaylord Production," announced the publisher's son, Edward K. Gaylord II, who popped up among the corn stalks to bring down the curtain on the $150-a-plate dinner for 600 people that raised $50,000 to help finance the Edward L. Gaylord Oklahoma City Chamber of Commerce Foundation.[14]

Lee Allan recognized the significance of Tinker Air Force Base to the economy in the Oklahoma City Metropolitan Area. He formed a special task force to make certain the goals of Tinker and its commanders were adopted by the chamber of commerce. Lee Allan gave special credit to chamber president Ed Cook for maintaining a healthy relationship between Oklahoma City and Tinker Air Force Base.

Major General Richard Burpee was commander of Tinker and joined Lee Allan's efforts. The first time Lee Allan met Burpee, Lee Allan asked, "What can we do to help you?" Burpee, who often had to escort distinguished visitors around

ABOVE: Lee Allan, left, as chairman of the Oklahoma City Chamber of Commerce, and Ray Ackerman don derbies for a Laurel and Hardy act at a Dining Out event at Tinker Air Force Base. They were introduced with a limerick, "Ray and Lee Allan like to party—selling ads, raising bucks, being arty—from a distance it seems, in one of our dreams—they resemble Laurel 'n Hardy."

the sprawling base in a hot, un-air conditioned military bus, said, "Could we get a good bus?"[15]

Lee Allan went into action and raised the money to purchase a used double-decker English-style touring bus. The bus, called the Tinker Trolley, was painted yellow and blue, the Tinker colors. The bus was air conditioned and equipped with an intercom system so hosts could comfortably talk to visitors without yelling.[16]

When the bus was dedicated, Burpee loaded dignitaries who had helped with the project onto the bus—but failed to notify Security Police that the bus was leaving the base. When officers stoppd the bus, John Kirkpatrick yelled, "We'll all be shot!" General Burpee stepped off the bus first and assured his security policeman that he had full control of the situation.[17]

In 1985, KTVY-TV continued to hold a strong position in the Oklahoma City television market, but was being strongly challenged by the two other network affiliated stations, KWTV and KOCO. It was not that KTVY-TV had lessened in quality, but the number and quality of its competitors had

Left to right, Lee Allan, entertainer Vince Gill, former OU football coach Barry Switzer, and former National Football League star and sportscaster Merlin Olsen, at the Vince Gill Golf Tournament in Oklahoma. Switzer says Lee Allan is a "finisher," he completes projects of which he dreams.

changed the station's share of the market. Cable television was also beginning to detract viewers from local stations.[18]

Lee Allan supported a strong local news presence with Jack Ogle, Ernie Shultz, George Tomek, Brad Edwards, and Linda Cavanaugh. Butch and Ben McCain hosted a popular morning show. Administrators and sales managers such as Tom Parrington, Art Garretson, Hudson Shubert, Wes Clanahan, and Nick Panos were strong and important to the station's success. Dan Bates was brought on board as assistant manager and Lee Allan named Bill Thrash as station manager. Jim Williams was a popular weatherman and Bob Barry continued to win awards as sports director.

Barry was highly recruited by KWTV in 1985. However, Lee Allan convinced Barry to consider a new longtime deal at KTVY that included the payment of lifetime annuities. But before Barry could sign a new contract, he suffered a heart attack and was told he needed bypass surgery. Lee Allan sent news director Ron Turner to Barry's hospital room the night before the surgery to have Barry sign the new contract. Turner said, "Sign this thing and if you die during the operation, the contract with its annuities goes into effect. If you make it, you can continue negotiations when you recover."[19]

Barry remembered, "Lee Allan was being more than a friend, because my wife would have been taken care of if I died during the operation."

Left to right, Lee Allan, President George W. Bush, and publisher Edward L. Gaylord visit during a tour of the Oklahoma City National Memorial.

Fortunately, Barry survived and continued his sports casting career.[20]

In 1987, Lee Allan invited and the Oklahoma City Chamber of Commerce hosted Vice President George Bush to privately brief business and government leaders on President Ronald Reagan's efforts to deregulate the oil and gas industry and its effects upon the banking industry. Oklahoma was still reeling from the failure of Penn Square Bank and the bust in the state's oil industry.

Bush, in Oklahoma City to raise money to finance his own campaign for the presidency, was receptive to ideas from Lee Allan

ABOVE: Lee Allan, DeAnn, and their three daughters relax at home.

and others, including Oklahoma City Mayor Ron Norick, retired banker J.W. McLean, banker William O. Johnstone, CMI Corporation president Bill Swisher, former Oklahoma Attorney General G.T. Blankenship, personnel service owner Terry Neese, and Dennis Howard of Oklahoma Farm Bureau.

LEFT: When University of Oklahoma running back Billy Sims was inducted into the College Football Hall of Fame, Lee Allan was in New York City with OU's two previous Heisman winners. Left to right, Steve Owens, Billy Sims, Lee Allan, and Billy Vessels.

After the meeting, Bush wrote Lee Allan, "It was a constructive and informative session and made me even more aware of the special problems facing your state."[21]

LEFT: Lee Allan, left, and longtime friend University of North Carolina basketball coach Dean Smith playing golf at Oak Tree Golf and Country Club. The two met in their college days.

LEFT: Lee Allan, at podium, honors publisher Edward L. Gaylord, at a charity roast promoted by Henry Zarrow in Tulsa in 1989. Lee Allan worked for Gaylord at WKY-Radio and WKY-TV for many years. They were always friends. But after Lee Allan left the broadcast stations, he and Gaylord became close friends and confidants. At the roast, Lee Allan said he was concerned that if his comments were too offensive to Gaylord, he might cut Lee Allan's pension from WKY, a whopping $85 a month.

BELOW: On the golf course. Left to right, Bob Barry, Dick Ellis, Lee Allan's brother, Dale Smith, and Lee Allan.

In the late 1980s, Oklahoma City officials began considering how to formally celebrate the centennial of the Land Run of 1889 that opened Oklahoma City to settlement. The Myriad Gardens was completed and development of Bricktown was underway. The Centennial Expressway was open, Remington Park was a major attraction—Oklahoma City was at the dawn of a new century.

At first, officials considered hosting a World's Fair. However, with the faltering economy and a history of other cities losing money on a World's Fair, Oklahoma City shelved that idea. The Economic Development Foundation of the Oklahoma City Chamber of Commerce took on the responsibility to organize the Land Run Centennial. G.T. Blankenship was presi-

Oklahoma Governor Henry Bellmon was a special guest at the Oklahoma City Chamber of Commerce dinner in which Lee Allan turned over the chairman's gavel to Clyde Ingle. Left to right, Bellmon, Ingle, Lee Allan, and Oklahoma City Mayor Ron Norick, who called Lee Allan "Oklahoma City's champion promoter" and a "genius" when it came to planning special events to celebrate the city's past and future.

dent and Paul Strasbaugh was executive vice president of the foundation.

Strasbaugh remembered, "We set out to secure a large national or international event." Oklahoma City successfully competed with several large cities such as Phoenix, Arizona; Minneapolis, Minnesota; and Pittsburgh, Pennsylvania for the right to hold the 1989 Olympic Festival.[22]

Oklahoma City prevailed and Oklahoma Centennial Sports, Inc., was organized to manage the festival. Lee Allan was asked to be the chairman and Clay Bennett was dubbed the president of what became the largest single event ever held in Oklahoma. He was assisted by Tim O'Toole, Pete Everest, Dick Parker, and thousands of volunteers.

The opening ceremony provided the audience with the thrill of a lifetime with former President Ronald Reagan and Bob Hope joining stars such as Vince Gill, Reba McEntire, James Garner, Roger Miller, and Patti Page. The mystery carrier of the Olympic torch was track star Florence Griffith Joyner (Flo Jo). Singers Ray Charles and Crystal Gayle headlined the closing ceremonies. Strasbaugh said, "Both the opening and closing ceremonies equaled what we see at the international Olympics."[23]

As he had done in producing the *Stars and Stripes Shows,* Lee Allan called upon his friends to host stars and take care of the myriad of details necessary to put on a huge extravaganza. Don Reynolds provided his personal custom airplane to bring President Reagan and Bob Hope to Oklahoma City. Lee Allan's friends opened their homes to visiting dignitaries.[24]

The opening ceremony at a jam-packed Memorial Stadium on the OU campus in Norman was spectacular. President Reagan and Hope landed on the track and field venue across the street from the football field in a helicopter provided by

ABOVE: Among the sports stars who appeared in an earlier *Stars and Stripes Show* were, left to right, OU and professional football players Dewey and Lucious Selmon, and Olympic gold medalist Wayne Wells.

UPPER RIGHT: Left to right, Lee Allan, Carol Hansen, Barry Switzer, Betty Jo Lemons, and Oklahoma City University President Tom McDaniel.

RIGHT: Lee Allan throws out the first ball for the 1989 U.S. Olympic Festival.

ABOVE: On a trip to look at University of Texas athletic facilities are, left to right, Lee Allan, Doug Switzer, Barry Switzer, Texas football coach Mack Brown, and Clay Bennett. Switzer and Lee Allan were like brothers. Switzer said, "He's always looking out for me. He genuinely cares about me as a friend. No one sticks by my side like Lee Allan. He even decorates my office."

UPPER LEFT: Baseball superstar Mickey Mantle, left, and Lee Allan visit prior to the Olympic Festival opening ceremonies.

LEFT: Oklahoma baseball superstar Mickey Mantle signs baseballs to be given to sponsors of Oklahoma City charity events. Lee Allan and Clay Bennett look on.

Herman Meinders. Ray Ackerman said, "No one else but Lee Allan could have pulled it off. He's our guy!"[25]

Lee Allan knew his long hours and sleepless nights had been worth it when he heard the story of a 10-year-old boy who looked up at his father after the ceremony and said, "Just think, Dad. I'm from Oklahoma!"[26]

BELOW: Lee Allan and DeAnn had time to stop by a novelty booth at Opryland Park in Nashville, Tennessee, to pose for their "cover" photograph.

THE READERS AND CRITICS POLL

ISSUE 510 • OCTOBER • U.K. i90 • $2.50

RollingStone

The Rock and Roll
Hall of Fame

ELVIS PRESLEY

TINA TURNER

BUDDY HOLLY

BIG BOPPER

THE BEATLES

JIMI HENDRIX

ELTON JOHN

ARTIST
of the
YEAR

ABOVE: At the opening of the Henry Freede Wellness Center on the Oklahoma City University campus are, left to right, Johnny Bench, Curt Gowdy, William Shdeed, Johnny Unitas, and Lee Allan.

Left to right, DeLee Smith. football star Terry Bradshaw, Jennifer Smith, and Wendy Smith at a Vince Gill Golf Tournament party.

Lee Allan was king of the Beaux Arts Ball in Oklahoma City in 2003. A decade earlier, he was inducted into the Oklahoma Hall of Fame, the highest honor the state can bestow upon one of its citizens.

The 1990s were filled with other awards for Lee Allan. In 1995, he was inducted, along with former *Today* host Jim Hartz of Tulsa, into the Oklahoma Association of Broadcasters Hall of Fame. He also was named a Pathmaker by the Oklahoma County Historical Society.

chapter twelve

Lee Allan has that mischievous grin on his face. He leans back in his chair and smiles—knowingly, conspiratorily—as if to say, wait until I share with you my special secret. His secrets are always special—always larger than life.

—FRANK KEATING

No one will ever know how many lives Lee Allan's projects have touched.

—ANGUS McQUEEN

Lee Allan's activities are inextricably intertwined with the growth and development of Oklahoma.

—CLAY BENNETT

OKLAHOMA EVENTS

I n 1987, *Knight-Ridder Broadcasting, Inc.,* which had recently purchased KTVY-TV, began replacing general managers at each of their five television properties. Even though Channel Four in Oklahoma City was doing well in ratings and revenue, Lee Allan knew his time at the station was short. He saw the handwriting on the wall when Knight-Ridder executive Dan Gold sent him a book that emphasized Harvard University and Stanford University, Gold's two alma maters.[1]

Lee Allan did not like Gold's decision to move him out of the top spot at KTVY-TV, but he understood Knight-Ridder's motives for putting its own management team in place. Lee Allan looked back on 31 years with WKY-Radio and Channel Four. He had enjoyed his decades in broadcasting, but also looked forward to new challenges. He considered his options and turned to his old friend, Edward L. Gaylord for advice.

Gaylord still owned WKY-Radio—presenting a certain job possibility for Lee Allan. However, Gaylord had ideas of creating his own advertising agency to represent the advertising interests of the Oklahoma Publishing Company and his other business concerns.[2]

To make a decision about whether to open an advertising agency, Lee Allan talked with Oklahoma City advertising executives Doc Jordan and Ray Ackerman, his longtime friend and co-worker in many civic projects. Ackerman had founded the state's largest advertising agency, at the time called Ackerman, Hood, & McQueen (Ackerman McQueen). Ackerman had semi-retired from day-to-day management of the agency but strongly believed Lee Allan should talk to Angus McQueen, the president of the firm.[3]

When they met, McQueen shared his vision with Lee Allan about how Ackerman McQueen might become more involved in community affairs and how Lee Allan, with his many contacts, could add to the agency's client list. McQueen said Lee Allan reminded him of his late father, Marvin McQueen, who with Ray Ackerman had built the advertising agency into one of the most respected firms of its kind in the nation.

After a series of talks, McQueen convinced Lee Allan to join forces with Ackerman McQueen in a unique way. In the beginning, Lee Allan was a senior vice president of the agency, but was allowed to take leave to work on the Olympic Festival in 1989. Within weeks of his arriving at Ackerman McQueen, Lee Allan was able to bring *The Daily Oklahoman* to the agency as an advertising customer.

On December 29, 1989, OK Events Inc. was formed as a subsidiary of the advertising agency. Bill Winkler, now the chief operating officer and chief financial officer of Ackerman McQueen, said, "It was a brilliant decision on the part of Angus McQueen to bring Lee Allan on board. He was different. A lot of people had great ideas in which they believed—but Lee Allan acted on the ideas and produced results."[4]

Lee Allan believed teaming up with Ackerman McQueen was the second of two pivotal career moves in his life. His initial break at WKY-Radio launched his career—now being able to expend his energies each day on projects for his hometown seemed like a dream.

Within a short time, Lee Allan's presence at OK Events produced new clients and additional revenue for Ackerman McQueen. In addition to the huge Oklahoma Publishing Company account, the agency began handling advertising for the Oklahoma Gas & Electric Company and Remington Park, the world-class horse racing venue in Oklahoma City. Observers believed Lee Allan's influence was vital in luring clients to Ackerman McQueen. There was no doubt that Lee Allan exerted incredible influence with the business and political leadership in Oklahoma's capital city.[5]

Lee Allan's departure from KTVY-TV left a void—but the move was good for Ackerman McQueen. Former Miss

America Jane Jayroe, who Lee Allan had hired as a news anchor at Channel Four after convincing her to return to her native Oklahoma from a highly lucrative anchor position in Dallas, Texas, wrote Lee Allan, "The loss of your leadership is costly both professionally and personally to so many fine people… myself included…However, it's obvious that your many skills will transfer well to an advertising agency."[6]

OK Events, commonly referred to as Oklahoma Events, was a natural progression of Lee Allan's unique promotional abilities that had begun during his college days at OU and had been perfected in the Air Force and in a quarter century as a radio and television executive.

Ackerman McQueen welcomed Lee Allan with open arms. Receptionist Sharyn Chesser remembered the first time Lee Allan walked in the door, "I looked up and saw this handsome man who had to be the friendliest person in the world. And, he was the same whether he was in the office or if you saw him in the grocery store. He never saw a stranger. He always had time for the little guy." Chesser said, "Lee Allan is a champion of speaking up for people who don't have a voice."[7]

Lee Allan, as president of OK Events Inc., was immediately accepted by the large professional staff at the advertising agency. "Lee Allan cared about our personal lives—our happiness and our sadness," Chesser said, "When my mother lost a leg, he constantly asked about her."[8]

Lee Allan's compassionate side would never allow him to intentionally hurt anyone's feelings. One day, he casually told a joke about a one-legged Iraqi dictator in the presence of Chesser, before he was aware of Chesser's mother's amputation. When he was told about the surgery, he was crushed, and apologized profusely for his remarks.[9]

Ray Ackerman said, "Lee Allan knows everybody—and he knows how to sell businessmen on the idea that bringing in a big celebrity to Oklahoma City was good for business and good for developing pride in Oklahoma."[10] Clay Bennett, who worked with Lee Allan on many major projects, said of his close friend, "He exploits, in a positive sense, any relationship with anyone he has known in his life. He is forever loyal to his causes, his family, high school, and college. In the end, everyone benefits from his efforts."[11]

Contacts that Lee Allan developed decades before producing the *Stars and Stripes Shows* were used to lure big name entertainers to Oklahoma City for charity and civic events. Bob Hope, Vince Gill, and many other superstars were only a phone call away for Lee Allan.

Left to right, singer Katrina Elam, Oklahoma Lieutenant Governor Mary Fallin, Lee Allan, and former Miss America Shawntel Smith Wuerch, at the annual Oklahoma Hall of Fame banquet.

At OK Events, Lee Allan was free to spend all his time putting together fund-raising drives for special projects. Oklahoma Publishing Company executive Ed Martin, later president of Ackerman McQueen, was a constant observer of Lee Allan's talents in the 1990s, "Every successful city has to have a Lee Allan. He's a great fundraiser, but a better description of what he does is 'project builder.'"[12]

Martin believes Lee Allan's sensitivity is what makes him a great expediter of worthy projects. Martin said, "He is sensitive to issues and the people involved in a project. He only takes on projects he believes in—I've seen him disappointed when someone said no to him. However, he accepts it with a smile and keeps moving forward."[13]

"Lee Allan's sensitivity to detail," said Jane Jayroe, "is what makes him the master planner of events. He just knows how to bring a 'wow' factor to events and yet be a stickler for the tiniest of details."[14] General Richard Burpee said, "He is a bulldog with a sensitive side—always caring about what is best for everyone involved. He is the most unselfish man I know."[15]

Lee Allan's growing friendship with Edward L. Gaylord added much luster to Lee Allan's ability to sell corporate and political leaders on projects. Often, Lee Allan and Gaylord discussed who might join them in funding a particular project. Martin said, "It was a positive for Lee Allan to be able to say that Mr. Gaylord was participating in the project."[16]

Throughout the 1990s and in the early years of the 21st century, Lee Allan was involved in virtually every major fund-raising project in Oklahoma City. Whether raising money for promoting Oklahoma City in print advertisements in the *Wall Street Journal,* keeping Tinker Air Force Base off Pentagon base closure lists, bringing Broadway plays or television comedian Jay

Leno to Oklahoma, booking professional sports teams for exhibition games in town, or hosting a tribute to former OU coach Bud Wilkinson, Lee Allan was in the "thick of the fight."[17]

Lee Allan got into the statue business when Gaylord became interested in funding a statue of former President Ronald Reagan for the National Cowboy and Western Heritage Museum in Oklahoma City. Lee Allan worked out the details for sculptor Glenna Goodacre of Santa Fe, New Mexico, to complete the Reagan statue which now greets visitors at the museum. A duplicate of the Reagan statue is located at the Reagan Presidential Library in California.

Working with Clayton I. "Clay" Bennett, Lee Allan expedited the completion of statues of former Governor Henry Bellmon, longtime chamber of commerce executive Paul Strasbaugh, and Gaylord for the state fairgrounds. In 2004, a duplicate of the Gaylord statue was placed on the University of Oklahoma campus in Norman at the new journalism building funded by the Gaylord family.

Lee Allan's fellow citizens recognized his greatness—his ability to take an idea and make it happen. Former Oklahoma Attorney General G.T. Blankenship said, "Lee Allan is the greatest civic leader Oklahoma City ever had."[18] Attorney Burns Hargis quipped, "I have often wondered what we would do in Oklahoma City without Lee Allan."[19] Banker H.E. "Gene" Rainbolt said, "Lee Allan has a great opening line when he wants you to contribute. He simply calls and says, 'I feel confident I've got something you'll be interested in!'"[20] American Floral Services founder Herman Meinders said, "When Lee Allan gets you interested, you end up feeling excited and happy you were given the chance to be part of the project!"[21] Clay Bennett said, "He serves a unique role in communicating his enthusiasm about a project. You know that his sincerity is purely about improving Oklahoma."[22]

Lee Allan's contributions were noted by New York Yankee star Bobby Murcer and his wife, Kay. They wrote, "Lee Allan is the real Santa Claus! Look at the comparison! A large, jolly man who brings joy and lots of gifts to everyone in the community. He's lovable, creative, has a tireless team of elves who assist with every magical production…and he knows the whereabouts of every person alive!"[23]

The special touch Lee Allan added to promotional events is legendary. One year when he was preparing for the kickoff luncheon for Festival of the Horse, a 10-day event at Remington Park to honor the horse industry in Oklahoma, he and DeAnn spotted old, worn-out cowboy boots at a garage sale. "The light bulb came on!" Lee Allan recalled. After a few more garage sale stops, he had purchased dozens of pairs of old cowboy boots he personally painted to be used as centerpieces for the Festival of the Horse luncheon.[24] Soon, planners of several events wanted to use the boots for centerpieces. Eventually, Lee Allan gave the boots to the National Cowboy and Western Heritage Museum for their use.

The Festival of the Horse evolved into the Vince Gill Celebrity Golf Tournament, which Lee Allan built into a major attraction. Participants contributed substantial sums to play golf with leaders in sports and entertainment to raise money for worthy causes.

In 1991, Lee Allan and OK Events organized a "Welcome Home" celebration for Oklahoma troops returning from Desert Storm. Lieutenant General Tom Kelly and Oklahoma-born comedian Argus Hamilton were guests at the state capitol event that displayed good, old fashioned patriotism and flag waving.

Lee Allan also played a major role in negotiations that resulted in a local group of Oklahoma City businessmen purchasing the Triple A minor league baseball franchise in Oklahoma City. The Oklahoma Publishing Company, furniture magnates Bill and Larry Mathis, and auto dealer Bob Moore led a group of 13 investors who paid $8 million for the baseball club from Jeffrey Loria of New York, now the owner of the NFL's Philadelphia Eagles.

The idea had begun with Gaylord expressing interest in keeping the minor league franchise in Oklahoma City locally-owned. One morning at breakfast, after hearing another rumor that the Oklahoma City franchise would be sold to out-of-state investors, Gaylord asked Lee Allan, "What are we going to do about it?"

After Gaylord told Lee Allan how much he was willing to invest, Lee Allan raised initial monies to keep minor league baseball in Oklahoma City. Gaylord's son-in-law, Clay Bennett, soon took over management of the baseball franchise which changed its name to the Oklahoma RedHawks. Bennett completed putting together the investment group that made the RedHawks' franchise successful.

When the world premiere of the movie, *My Heroes Have Always Been Cowboys,* was hosted by E.K. Gaylord II and Martin Poll at the Penn Square Mall theater in Oklahoma City in 1991, Willie Nelson, the Oak Ridge Boys, James Stewart, Scott Glenn, Kate Capshaw, Gary Bussey, and Wilford Brimley made special appearances. Lee Allan and OK Events planned and executed the program.

In 1992, Lee Allan made Oklahoma City "a major league city" for at least one night. For decades, professional sports teams had played exhibition games in the city, but Lee Allan was able to convince the Edmonton Oilers and New York Islanders to play a regular season National Hockey League game at the Myriad Convention Center. It was the first time a regular season game for a major league sports franchise had been played in Oklahoma City. Lee Allan's contact list made the difference. He got the idea for the regular season game when he read that the former assistant director of the opening ceremonies of the 1989 Olympic Festival, had become manager of National Hockey League Properties.

The event was a huge success, convincing Lee Allan that Oklahoma City could someday support a major league hockey or basketball franchise.[25] Columnist Max Nichols, writing in *The Journal Record,* said, "This is a major coup for Smith in the ongoing effort to develop a national image of a 'class act' for Oklahoma City in staging major entertainment events of this kind."[26]

Lee Allan told a reporter, "I'm interested in having facilities and venues that look to the future. If we can get major league franchises to consider Oklahoma City, and attract college basketball tournaments, I can see hotels and restaurants being added to support the events."[27] Lee Allan's vision was clear, years before the improvements of the MAPS Projects became a reality.

In 1993, Lee Allan used his quiet professionalism to secure the booking of the Tony Award-winning *Will Rogers Follies,* starring Keith Carradine, at Oklahoma City's Civic Center Music Hall. While the show was still in rehearsal and before it opened on Broadway in New York City, Lee Allan recognized that a public relations bonanza was available to promote Oklahoma's down home virtues and wholesome goodness. Joe Carter, director of the Will Rogers Memorial in Claremore at the time, said, "Lee Allan convinced producers of the show to come to

Oklahoma during a tough competitive time when every enlightened theater across the land was bidding hard for the show."[28]

Again, it was some of Lee Allan's long list of Oklahoma connections that allowed him to bring *Will Rogers Follies* to Oklahoma City. The co-producer of the show was Max Weitzenhoffer, a veteran Broadway producer who grew up in Oklahoma City. After the successful run of the show in Oklahoma City, Lee Allan said, "It was good cheer and positive public imagery that Oklahoma needs badly and that money could not buy."[29] Lee Allan was elated that all eight shows of *Will Rogers Follies* were sold out, a result of the professional production of Lee Allan and OK Events.

Because the Oklahoma Publishing Company was a major backer of the Oklahoma production of the *Will Rogers Follies,* Lee Allan convinced designers to replace the name of a major national newspaper on a set backdrop announcing the deaths of Rogers and Wiley Post to the *Oklahoma City Times.*
National Basketball Association exhibition games were well received in Oklahoma City. Lee Allan and his staff worked with the front offices of the New York Knicks, San Antonio Spurs, Phoenix Suns, and Detroit Pistons to give Oklahoma basketball fans the opportunity to see NBA stars such as Charles Barkley, Patrick Ewing, David Robinson, and Grant Hill.

"Whether an event was a $1,000 or $1 million deal, it was a 'big deal' for Lee Allan," remembered Ctaci Combs, who worked alongside Lee Allan at OK Events from 1990 to 1997. "Regardless of the budget," Combs said, "he always added the finest of details—from hot air and helium balloons to red-white-blue bunting—from flyovers to free falls to fireworks—from confetti to cheerleaders—from maestros to marching bands."[30]

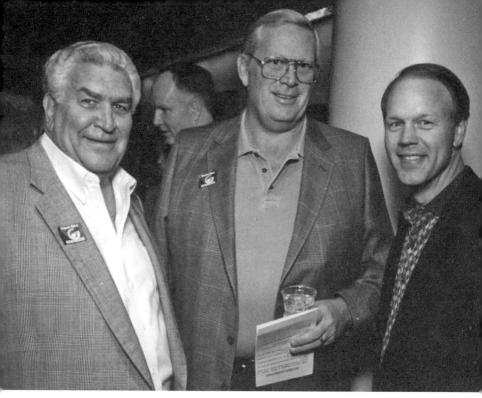

Lee Allan was famous for his Oklahoma hospitality. During the annual Vince Gill Golf Tournament, Combs, and Lee Allan's middle daughter, Jennifer, set an Oklahoma theme around the golf course with barbecue, corn-on-the-cob, pork sandwiches, and incredible desserts. Shortly after OK Events was formed, Jennifer began working for her father. Within a few years, her two sisters, DeLee and Wendy also joined the OK Events Staff. Jennifer said, "He's the kindest, most compassionate father in the world—but he expects results from his employees, including his three girls."[31]

Lee Allan's friendship with stars has more than once resulted in funny stories in the OK Events office. Many of Lee Allan's "normal" friends often called, pretending to be Bob Hope or some famous star. One day, however, Ctaci Combs thought the male caller was pretending to be Vince Gill. When Gill said, "This is Vince Gill," she replied, "Yeah, and I'm Princess

UPPER LEFT: Lee Allan, left, with Williams Companies president Keith Bailey, center, and Oklahoma United States Senator Don Nickles at the Vince Gill Celebrity Golf Tournament. Bailey said, "Lee Allan has a way of making good things happen—quickly and professionally."

ABOVE: Larry Nichols, left, and Lee Allan when Nichols was presented the Tribute to Excellence Award by the Arthritis Foundation.

RIGHT: Lee Allan, Mex Frates, and Ray Ackerman were active in leadership of the Oklahoma Heritage Association.

Diana!" When Combs realized the country music star was really on the phone, she walked red-faced into Lee Allan's office and announced it was Gill.[32]

In the 1990s, Lee Allan publicly exhorted city leaders to build new sports venues, including a huge arena that he saw as a key to attracting big-league sports to Oklahoma City. He threw his support behind Oklahoma City Mayor Ron Norick and the Oklahoma City Chamber of Commerce-backed plan called MAPS, an acronym for Metropolitan Area Projects. Lee Allan was active in the advertising campaign to convince taxpayers to approve an increase in sales tax to fund a massive redevelopment effort of downtown Oklahoma City. He produced an excitement-building program at the Myriad Convention Center for MAPS supporters.

During the next decade, nearly one billion dollars was spent for construction of the state-of-the-art baseball field for the Oklahoma RedHawks; renovation of the Civic Center Music Hall; construction of the Ford Center, a 20,000-seat all-purpose arena; renovation of the Myriad Convention Center, renamed the Cox Business Services Convention Center; improvements to the State Fairgrounds; construction of a new library/learning center complex; and construction of the Bricktown Canal, transforming the Bricktown area just east of downtown Oklahoma City into a commercial and restaurant mecca.

Lee Allan was instrumental in obtaining a major contribution to the construction of the new minor league baseball park from Southwestern Bell Telephone Company. Dave Lopez was the new Oklahoma vice president of Southwestern Bell. Lopez remembered, "He came to us at just the right time. I was interested in sports and our company was a part owner of the San Antonio Spurs. Lee Allan went the extra mile to make us happy, including the right to name the ballpark the Southwestern Bell Bricktown Ballpark."[33] When the telephone company changed its corporate name, the name of the ballpark was changed to SBC Bricktown Ballpark.

Lee Allan's heart was broken when the Alfred P. Murrah Federal Building was bombed on April 19, 1995. Along with other civic leaders, he did everything possible to draw the people of Oklahoma together to support the families of the 168 persons who died in the tragedy. When the Oklahoma City National Memorial was being organized, Lee Allan raised money to keep its staff intact. Memorial director Kari Watkins said, "He looked at the whole picture and helped us develop a plan to grow the memorial into a major and worthy attraction to honor the victims of the bombing."[34]

Lee Allan and OK Events provided media attention for the idea of a promotion called "168 Days," in which one victim was honored each day for the 168 days preceding the formal dedication of the Oklahoma City National Memorial in 2000. The idea was developed by Jeanette Elliott at Ackerman McQueen. Lee Allan met with officials of the Oklahoma Association of Broadcasters and sold them on the idea to get behind the promotion to honor the bombing victims. Tragically, Lee Allan's meeting with broadcasters was on the same day a devastating tornado hit Oklahoma City.

In 1996, Lee Allan raised money to pay for a huge sculpture of Oklahoma baseball legend Mickey Mantle to be placed at the third base entrance to the SBC Bricktown Ballpark. The unveiling of the statue was a huge celebration. Lee Allan invited Mantle's widow, Merlyn, and their sons, David and Danny. A host of former Yankee stars and other former major leaguers also attended the event, including Yogi Berra, Whitey

Ford, Tony Kubek, Mickey Tettleton, Enos Slaughter, Cot Deal, Ralph Terry, Eddie Fisher, Tom Sturdivant, Cal McLish, Gil McDougald, Jerry Lumpe, Bobby Morgan, Bobby Murcer, Gene Stephens, Norm Siebern, Bobby Richardson, Moose Skowron, Hank Bauer, and Ralph Houk.

Oklahoma RedHawks president Clay Bennett was master of ceremonies at a dinner at the Beacon Club honoring Mantle's teammates and other Oklahoma-connected major league stars in town for the occasion. ESPN sports announcer Roy Firestone provided the entertainment for the evening. OK Events arranged for each of Mantle's former teammates to place their handprints in clay at the base of the Mantle statue.

Former New York Yankees stars Bill "Moose" Skowron," left, and Hank Bauer, right, pose with Lee Allan at the Mickey Mantle Golf Tournament at the Shangri-La Resort in northeast Oklahoma.

BELOW: "Hollywood" Lee Allan, at left in sunglasses, visits with daughter, Jennifer Smith, center, and actor John Forsythe at a Festival of the Horse luncheon. Lee Allan was not trying to look like an actor—he had actually awakened that morning with pink eye.

At the unveiling of the Mantle statue, Dave Lopez realized that even though technology had changed the way business was conducted in the world, relationships still mattered. Lee Allan had used Mantle's relationship with his former teammates to draw them to Oklahoma City. Lopez, who felt like "a kid whose baseball card collection had come alive," sat with Whitey Ford, Yogi Berra, and Bobby Richardson at the unveiling. The players were talking about how grateful they were that Lee Allan had brought all the former Yankees back together. Berra said, "Lee Allan Smith does things right!"[35]

In 1998, Lee Allan and Ed Gaylord suggested over lunch at Boyd House with OU President David Boren that the university hire former Big Eight Commissioner Chuck Neinas to help select an athletic director, and ultimately, a new head football coach. OU football, one of the most gloried college gridiron programs in the country, had fallen on hard times—a fact that Lee Allan and thousands of other Sooner fans found hard to swallow.

OU hired Joe Castiglione from the University of Missouri as the new director of athletics. Shortly after Castiglione arrived in Norman, everyone kept telling him, "You need to meet

Lee Allan annually flew to New York City for the National Football League Foundation dinner. Left to right, OU athletic director Joe Castiglione, OU president David L. Boren, Lee Allan, and Billy Vessels, OU's first Heisman Trophy winner.

Lee Allan Smith!" Castiglione took the advice and asked for a meeting with Lee Allan. A bond of friendship was immediately established. Castiglione remembered, "From the moment I met him, I knew he loved OU and would do anything to better the university."[36]

Because Castiglione was new to Oklahoma, Lee Allan handed him a videotape of an hour-long pride-in-Oklahoma television program produced by Ackerman McQueen for the Oklahoma Department of Tourism and the Oklahoma Heritage Association, of which Lee Allan was elected president in 1999. Lee Allan had raised the money to fund the production of the program. Castiglione said, "By the time I had watched the tape, I was already proud to be an Oklahoman! Lee Allan's sincere love for Oklahoma had begun rubbing off on me."[37]

Castiglione called upon Lee Allan to rejuvenate a $100 million capital campaign for the OU athletic department. Regent G.T. Blankenship, a longtime friend of Lee Allan, encouraged his participation. With the help of the OU Board of Regents and President Boren, the Campaign for Sooner Sports—Great Expectations was a huge success.

Lee Allan played an integral role in working out details for the Gaylord family to make the largest gift in the history of OU to complete a $75 million expansion of the football stadium. Money raised in the program also made possible the Everest Training Center, the Freede Sports Medicine Center, and improvements to many sports venues on the OU campus.

In October, 2000, Lee Allan announced the successful completion of a fund raising drive that quickly had become close to his heart. Lee Allan orchestrated a spectacular banquet at the National Cowboy and Western Heritage Museum that featured the singing of Vince Gill, Amy Grant, and Reba

McEntire, accompanied by the Oklahoma City Philharmonic Orchestra, to announce that $4 million had been raised to build a new facility for Special Care, a home for children with special needs co-founded by Pam Newby and Joe Dan Trigg.

Lee Allan had persuaded the Oklahoma Publishing Company, Southwestern Bell Telephone Company, American Airlines, and many other companies and individuals

Special Care capital campaign chairmen Lee Allan, left, and Ed Martin, right, with Pam Newby, executive director, and Joe Dan Trigg, board chairman, at the groundbreaking for the new $4 million facility.

Left to right, Lee Allan, Amy Grant, Vince Gill, and Jennifer Smith in New York City at a special Williams Companies event produced by OK Events. The Tulsa Company hired OK Events to orchestrate publicity around a new public stock offering.

to sponsor the private concert for those who had contributed to the success of the fund raising drive.[38] Lee Allan sold tables for the event for up to $25,000 each. Additional monies had been raised by the Vince Gill Golf Tournament.

The new Special Care building was constructed at Northwest 122nd Street and North Western Avenue in Oklahoma City. Special Care executive director Pam Newby said, "Lee Allan put his heart and soul into our cause and made it super successful. His tender heart was challenged by the special kids we were trying to help."[39] Joe Dan Trigg, Special Care board president at the time of the fund-raising drive, said, "The project would have been impossible without Lee Allan's help!"[40] To honor Lee Allan's efforts for Special Care, the group placed a special plaque in the memorial garden of the Special Care center.

RIGHT: This photograph of Bob Stoops' announcement as the new coach of the University of Oklahoma football team featured Lee Allan and former coach Barry Switzer behind Stoops. The photograph, taken by *Oklahoman* photographer David McDaniel, appeared in media publications across the country.

Lee Allan and OU football coach Bob Stoops, right, at a Fellowship of Christian Athletes dinner, Stoops' first speech in Oklahoma following his selection to lead the Sooners.

ABOVE: Lee Allan loves OU football. At a NFL Foundation banquet in New York City, he talks with former OU quarterback and legendary University of Texas coach Darrell Royal, left, and Steve Owens, who won the Heisman Trophy as a Sooner running back in 1969. Royal said of Lee Allan, "He's always working for others." Owens knows Lee Allan's sensitive side. When Owens lost his son, the first call of condolence came from Lee Allan.

ABOVE: Lee Allan congratulates James "Jim" Harlow, left, upon his induction into the Oklahoma Hall of Fame, sponsored by the Oklahoma Heritage Association (OHA). After Harlow's death, Lee Allan raised $1 million to establish a chair in Harlow's name in ethics and business at the University of Oklahoma. While president of OHA, Lee Allan engineered the effort to secure a gift from Edward L. Gaylord to purchase the former Mid-Continent Life Insurance Building in Oklahoma for the Oklahoma Heritage Center, which will house the Oklahoma Hall of Fame. At center is Noble Foundation executive director John Snodgrass who knew Lee Allan at the Phi Gam house during their college days at OU.

RIGHT: Lee Allan and DeAnn treasure vacation time with friends in San Diego, California. Left to right, Dee Sadler, Margaret Short, George Short, Beth Ann Sadler, Lee Allan, and DeAnn.

LEFT: Lee Allan spent much of his time in the 1990s and early 21st century working on projects involving the University of Oklahoma. Left to right, OU president David L. Boren, Lee Allan, Libby Blankenship, and longtime OU regent G.T. Blankenship.

RIGHT: Lee Allan, left, and Keith Jackson, when the former University of Oklahoma tight end was inducted into the College Football Hall of Fame.

FAR RIGHT: Clay Bennett, left, Barry Switzer, and Lee Allan at Switzer's induction into the College Football Hall of Fame. Of Lee Allan Switzer said, "He makes ideas come to life. Oklahoma is so lucky to have him. He is much more than a great public servant, he makes our lives better."

BELOW: Lee Allan brought *The Tonight Show* host Jay Leno for a concert at Oklahoma City's Civic Center Music Hall. Left to right, Lee Allan, DeLee Smith, Leno, and Jennifer Smith.

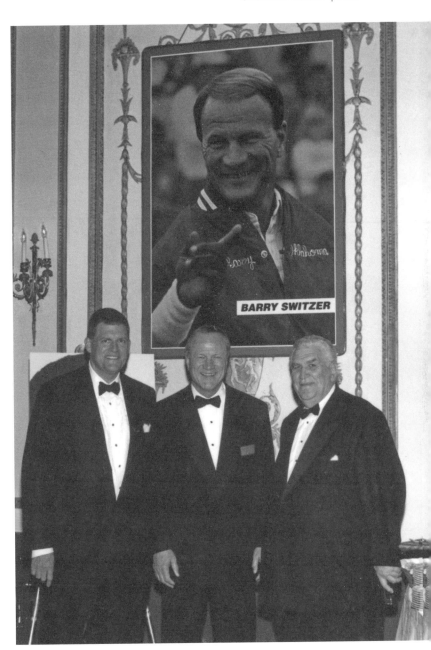

chapter thirteen

If you have something to be done, and you're sure you want it done on a grand scale—Lee Allan's the guy.

—JOE CASTIGLIONE

When his time comes, God will give him a gold telephone and an 800 number so he can still help people.

—SUGAR SMITH

He never forgot the teaching of his mother—with a smile, he gets things done for the good of many.

—LEE STIDHAM

Lee Allan elevates the game for the rest of us.

—DAVE LOPEZ

THE NEW CENTURY

Lee Allan, right, and contractor James Pickel worked closely in orchestrating the reopening of Oklahoma City's Civic Center Music Hall in 2001 and were featured in a *Friday* story about the grand event. Courtesy *Friday*.

In April, 2001, Lee Allan's friends gathered at Gaillardia Golf and Country Club in Oklahoma City to honor and roast him. The black-tie sellout was a major fundraiser for the Oklahoma Chapter of the Arthritis Foundation who gave Lee Allan the Tribute to Excellence Award. Master of ceremonies Burns Hargis showed no mercy on Lee Allan. Peggy Gandy, writing in *The Daily Oklahoman*, said,

"Hargis placed Smith on a slow-turning skewer as he turned up the heat with his one-liners."[1]

Hargis appropriately began the evening, "Welcome to Lee Allan Smith's roast; for an event this size we really need an industrial-size grill."[2] When Hargis asked the audience if anyone was present who had not been called by Lee Allan to contribute, no hands were raised. Edward L. Gaylord and Barry Switzer were among the roasters.

To Lee Allan (and the Girls!). To
well done! you're the Best!

The City of
OKLAHOMA CITY

Mayor Kir

September 11, 2001

Oklahoma City Mayor Kirk Humphreys and the city council called upon Lee Allan to orchestrate the reopening of the Civic Center Music Hall in September, 2001. The project included selling suites, naming rights, and seating packages. Lee Allan escorted potential donors through hard hat areas and around wet concrete. City Manager Jim Couch said, "He created an image in everyone's mind about how great this facility was going to be and how they should financially support it."[3]

On the second evening of the grand opening, an Oklahoma downpour hit. Rain was not in the forecast, so many patrons arrived drenched. Just as a Michael Feinstein-Jimmy Webb performance with the Oklahoma City Philharmonic Orchestra began, lightning struck a transformer and knocked out all power except for emergency lighting. City Manager Couch remembered, "Lee Allan met back stage with the performers and insisted that the weather would not ruin everyone's evening."[4]

Lee Allan and Mayor Humphreys appeared together on stage. Without a microphone, Lee Allan used his booming voice to ask the 2,500 people to be patient. The mayor was upbeat and encouraged the crowd to "have a great and unique evening."

On the morning of September 11, 2001, Lee Allan and his staff at OK Events gathered for a photograph with Oklahoma City Mayor Kirk Humphreys to celebrate the reopening of the Civic Center Music Hall. While at the mayor's office, the World Trade Center was attacked by terrorists. Lee Allan joined the mayor in watching the horrible events of that morning on television. Left to right, Jennifer Smith, Lee Allan, Mayor Humprheys, DeLee Smith, and Julie Huff.

Webb and Feinstein performed without sound, under the light of a flashlight, until power was restored. Couch said, "It was a wonderful evening that patrons continue to remember as the best performance they ever attended."[5] Lee Allan stood at the door at the end of the show and thanked everyone for attending.

One of Lee Allan's most visible projects in the early years of the new millennium was the dedication of the new dome atop the State Capitol in Oklahoma City. The original design plans for the Capitol called for a dome—but funding problems and shortages of iron during World War I caused the state legislature to scrap the plan, leaving the Capitol ceiling unfinished.

In 2001, construction on a new dome began. Most of the $21 million was private funds, raised in an effort led by Governor Frank Keating and Ed Cook. The dome was completed in the fall of 2002 and dedication ceremonies were planned for Statehood Day, November 16. For one year before the dedication, Lee Allan and the OK Events staff worked tirelessly to make the dedication the greatest single celebration in Oklahoma history.

Governor Keating said, "Lee Allan didn't just plan a show, he planned and executed an extravaganza. His was greater than Operation Sail when we rededicated the Statue of Liberty. It was better than a Fourth of July on Washington Mall."[6]

The sky was filled with the largest Oklahoma fireworks display ever. The lineup of celebrities marking the occasion was unprecedented. Vince Gill served as master of ceremonies for a program that included a traveling cast of *The Music Man*, Bryan White, Amy Grant, Johnny Bench, Bobby Murcer, Leona Mitchell, the Ambassadors Choir, the Canterbury Choir, the OU and OSU pom squads, and Jimmy Webb. The evening was punctuated with an Air Force jet flyover. Keating remembered,

"It turned out to be a bright moment of Oklahoma history, an uplift to our people and our confidence. It was larger and better than any of us could have dreamed of."[7]

A huge crowd gathered around the Capitol to witness the event and tens of thousands more joined the celebration on live television. Lee Allan and Oklahoma Education Television Authority (OETA) deputy director of programming and production, Bill Thrash; Six Flags Corporation under the able leadership of Gary Story; David Thomas of Silvertree Productions; and Steve Dahlem were co-producers of the live television broadcast. For its coverage of the dedication, OETA and Lee Allan received a regional Emmy Award.

Burns Hargis, recognizing Lee Allan's contributions to Oklahoma, and his magnificent production of the dome dedication, quipped, "We should have put a statue of Lee Allan atop the dome—with his hand out!"[8]

Lee Allan is appreciated by his fellow Oklahomans. Marion DeVore said, "We are greatly blessed that Lee Allan was born in Oklahoma and stayed here!"[9] Robert Naifeh said, "Without his gifts, the growth and success of Oklahoma would have been slower achieved."[10]

A typical comment about Lee Allan's abilities came from Oklahoma Superintendent of Public Instruction Sandy Garrett, "He connects the dots and brings people together. He takes time to mentor new members of boards and commissions."[11] Attorney Mike Turpen said, "He has a positive influence on everyone he meets. He has made a difference in Oklahoma—he has left the woodpile higher than he found it."[12]

Dave Maloney, vice president of university development at OU, said Lee Allan "belongs to the people and traditions of the state of Oklahoma. There is no one who can visualize, raise funds, promote, and produce a special event to showcase any aspect of our state the way Lee Allan does."[13] Lee Allan's friend from college days, Eddie Crowder, said, "Lee Allan has the biggest heart in Oklahoma!"[14]

Lee Allan also impressed new leaders coming onto the scene in Oklahoma City. When Charles "Chuck" Schroeder, another fraternity connection for Lee Allan, became executive director of the National Cowboy and Western Heritage Museum, formerly the National Cowboy Hall of Fame, he heard of Lee Allan's reputation for raising money and orchestrating huge events. Schroeder, also a Phi Gam, scheduled a meeting with Lee Allan, and found his reputation was correct. Schroeder said, "He helped me weigh a project's feasibility and give me a feel of how the project would be perceived by the community.

Lee Allan looks over a script with, left to right, Vince Gill, Reba McEntire, and her husband and manager, Narvel Blackstock.

Lee Allan and DeAnn were close friends with Edward L. and Thelma Gaylord. When Gaylord died in 2003, Lee Allan said, "I don't think there has been or will be anyone like him. He was a giant of our time."

It is invaluable to be able to talk frankly with him in a trusting environment. I know I can be open with him without worrying about political ramifications."[15]

Lee Allan lost his closest friend when Edward L. Gaylord died in 2003. It was an honor for Lee Allan to assist in the memorial service for Gaylord at the National Cowboy and Western Heritage Museum. Elected and civic leaders called Gaylord a friend, a great wit, and generous philanthropist.

ABOVE: Lee Allan and his girls at Smithdale, a cabin in Colorado owned by Lee Allan's brother, Dale, and his wife, Ann.

RIGHT: Lee Allan, and his good buddy, former Heisman Trophy winner Steve Owens, right, on the golf course.

585

ABOVE: Lee Allan pays tribute to Oklahoma City native Joe Carter, the star of the 1993 World Series. At left is Oklahoma City Councilwoman Willa Johnson.

Lee Allan commissioned a statue of Oklahoma baseball great Johnny Bench for the SBC Bricktown Ballpark in Oklahoma City. In this photograph, Bench, on ladder, inspects the casting with Lee Allan, left, and sculptor Paul Moore.

The past and present of OU football. Left to right, former OU player and University of Texas coach Darrell Royal, OU coach Bob Stoops, and Lee Allan stand in front of a portrait of former OU coach Bud Wilkinson, at an NFL Foundation dinner in New York City.

RIGHT: At the foot of the finished Johnny Bench statue are, left to right, Wendy Smith, Bench, Lee Allan, and Jennifer Smith.

During the burial service, Lee Allan's cell phone began ringing. Jim Everest remembered, "The look of horror on his face was priceless as he unsuccessfully attempted to turn the phone off with everyone looking at him." The call was from someone taking care of last minute details for the memorial service. Everest said no one was upset, "We all knew Lee Allan was Ed's closest friend and we know Ed would have gotten a chuckle out of what happened."[16]

Many of Lee Allan's days since 2003 have been spent planning the celebration of Oklahoma's Centennial in 2007. Working with J. Blake Wade, executive

director of the Oklahoma Capitol Complex and Centennial Commemoration Commission, Lee Allan prepared a long list of projects that would make Oklahomans proud of celebrating a century of statehood.

Lee Allan's efforts have been perceived as being concentrated in Oklahoma City, but he works on many statewide projects. Tulsa's leading promoter, Larry Payton of Celebrity Attractions, said, "If you need things done in Oklahoma, and done right, you call Lee Allan. He is more than willing to work on projects outside Oklahoma City. I believe he really loves all of Oklahoma."[17]

Lee Allan was able to enlist OU football coach Bob Stoops to speak at a luncheon in Lawton honoring soldiers returning to

LEFT: Lee Allan, left, is honored by Oklahoma Governor Frank Keating after Lee Allan produced a world-class dedication of a new dome atop the Oklahoma State Capitol.

UPPER LEFT: Lee Allan, with the help of Angus McQueen and the National Rifle Association, was able to bring actor Charlton Heston, left, and wife, Lydia, to a celebration at the National Cowboy and Western Heritage Museum in 2003 for the unveiling of a statue of Heston. It was the last public appearance for the famed actor.

RIGHT: Left to right, John Michael Williams, Carolyn Hill, and Lee Allan were award winners at the 2003 Downtown Oklahoma City Incorporated banquet. Lee Allan was presented the Dean A. McGee Award for a lifetime of excellence, achievements, and involvement in downtown Oklahoma City.

BELOW: The Smiths and the Corbetts for dinner at Joe's Stone Crab in Miami Beach, Florida, during a trip to the 2001 Orange Bowl when OU won the national college football championship. Left to right, Kerr-McGee Chairman Luke Corbett, Carrie Corbett, Wendy Smith, Lee Allan, DeAnn, and Becky Corbett.

LOWER RIGHT: Jennifer Smith, left, and Wendy Smith visit with Kevin Costner at the 1998 Academy Awards in Hollywood, California.

Fort Sill from duty in Iraq. The benefit luncheon for the National Army Museum of the Southwest, a project of the

Centennial Commission, was scheduled one week before OU's 2003 season opener. Stoops had a firm rule that he never made public appearances the week before the season began. However, he made an exception for the cause—and Stoops was glad he did. In his remarks, he told the soldiers that he had taped up newspaper photos of American soldiers in the OU locker room and told his players, "Some people call OU football players heroes—but America's soldiers are our true heroes!"[18]

"Lee Allan is the creative energy and the drive behind the Centennial," J. Blake Wade said, "He does it all—envisions projects, raises the funds for them, and designs the groundbreakings and dedications."[19]

From April, 2003, to April, 2005, Lee Allan raised more than $10 million in private funds for Centennial commemoration

RIGHT: Visiting OU football coach Bob Stoops, right, are Lee Allan, Jim Everest, and Edward L. Gaylord. The OU football stadium was later named the Gaylord Family Memorial Stadium.

BELOW: OU President David L. Boren presented Lee Allan with a special ring in 2003, in appreciation of Lee Allan's efforts for the university.

projects. Among the projects that will help celebrate the state's 100th birthday are the Oklahoma Land Run Monument, a 365-foot bronze sculpture by Paul Moore that contains 45 heroic-size pieces and will span the Bricktown Canal; Oklahoma entries in the 2005-2007 Macy's Thanksgiving Day and the 2007 Tournament of Roses parade; a huge parade in downtown Oklahoma City on October 7, 2007; and a Centennial gala on November 16, 2007, that will top any previous celebration in Oklahoma history.

The new Oklahoma History Center was dedicated in November, 2005; the Native American Cultural Center will open in 2007; the revitalization of Lincoln Boulevard is an ongoing process; and a variety of celebrations that range from major league exhibition games to an Oklahoma State Fair Expo will happen in 2007, thanks to the energy of Lee Allan and a

Lee Allan, center, is congratulated on receiving the Governor's Arts Award by Joan Maguire, left, and Betty Price, director of the Oklahoma Arts Council.

LEFT: In 2004, former Beaux Arts kings gathered for a reunion photograph. Left to right, Dick Clements, Jim Everest, Tom Dulaney, and Sidney Upsher. Lee Allan is sitting. All are Phi Gams.

host of helpers. In 2005, the St. Louis Cardinals and Baltimore Orioles played two exhibition games before sold-out SBC Bricktown Ballpark crowds.

No doubt other projects will come to Lee Allan's mind in the middle of a meal or during the night. Wade said, "He's always thinking, always creating. I get calls from Lee Allan seven days a week, any time, day or night. Sometimes late at night the phone will ring, and it will be Lee Allan with another great idea."[20]

Edward C. Joullian, III, Lee Allan's friend and fellow lover of ice cream since Harding Junior High School days, said, "Lee Allan will forever have great ideas. You can hardly drive through Oklahoma City without seeing proof of his work."[21]Attorney Bill Robinson, of whom Lee Allan has bounced many of his

In September, 2004, Burns Hargis, left, was honored at the Dean A. McGee Awards. Congratulating Hargis are Lee Allan and Oklahoma State University mens basketball coach Eddie Sutton, right.

ideas over the years, said, "You have to credit him with persever-ance coupled with the ability to deliver."[22]

William E. "Bill" Durrett, senior chairman of American Fidelity Insurance Company, has known Lee Allan since high school. Durrett, who followed Lee Allan as chairman of the Oklahoma City Chamber of Commerce, predicted that a half dozen people would be required someday to replace Lee Allan's promotional efforts once Lee Allan has put on his last show on earth. Durrett said, "No doubt Lee Allan will be producing all the major celebrations in heaven."[23]

After the Centennial celebration, Lee Allan will move on to other projects. He is driven by a lifetime love for Oklahoma City and possesses an uncommon combination of preserving past memories and building for future generations. He never stops dreaming—and the lives of all citizens of his beloved Oklahoma are made better by his efforts.

The Lee Allan Smith family in 2005. Left to right, DeAnn, Lee Allan, DeLee, Wendy, Jennifer, and Fritz.

Notes

one | **a loving family**

1. *Shawnee News* (Shawnee, Oklahoma), November 5, 1914.
2. Interview with Lee Allan Smith January 26, February 10, February 17, and March 8, 2004, Archives, Oklahoma Heritage Association, Oklahoma City, Oklahoma, hereafter referred to as Heritage Archives. The collective interviews are hereafter referred to as Lee Allan Smith interview.
3. Bob Burke and Von Russell Creel, *Lyle Boren: Rebel Congressman* (Oklahoma City: Oklahoma Heritage Association, 1991), p. 30.
4. Roy P. Stewart and Pendleton Woods, *Born Grown: An Oklahoma City History* (Oklahoma City: Fidelity Bank, 1974), p. xvi, hereafter referred to as *Born Grown.*
5. Ibid., p. 212.
6. Ibid., p. 234.
7. Lee Allan Smith interview.
8. Ibid.
9. Ibid.
10. Interview with Curt Gowdy, March 15, 2004, Heritage Archives.
11. Lee Allan Smith interview.
12. Ibid.
13. Ibid.
14. Ibid.
15. Interview with Alfred Dewitt "Dee" Sadler, Jr., February 3, 2004, hereafter referred to as Dee Sadler interview, Heritage Archives.
16. Undated newspaper story, *The Daily Oklahoman,* Heritage Archives.
17. Interview with B.C. Clark, Jr., January 20, 2004, Heritage Archives.

two | **making friends**

1. Interview with Richard "Dick" Ellis, January 23, 2004, hereafter referred to as Dick Ellis interview, Heritage Archives.
2. Lee Allan Smith interview.
3. Ibid.
4. Interview with Randy Everest, March 10, 2004, hereafter referred to as

Randy Everest interview, Heritage Archives.
5. Dee Sadler interview.
6. Ibid.
7. Interview with Mary Katherine "Coca" Bell, January 14, 2004, hereafter referred to as Coca Bell interview, Heritage Archives.
8. Interview with Joe Dan Trigg, April 16, 2004, hereafter referred to as Joe Dan Trigg interview, Heritage Archives.
9. Dee Sadler interview.
10. Interview with Edwin "Ed" de Cordova, January 23, 2004, hereafter referred to as Ed de Cordova interview, Heritage Archives.
11. Lee Allan Smith interview.
12. Ibid.
13. Handwritten letter from Lee Allan Smith to Florence Smith, May 10, 1939, Heritage Archives.
14. Nadie Smith interview.
15. Lee Allan Smith interview.
16. Ibid.

three | **boomer sooner**
1. Lee Allan Smith interview.
2. Ibid.
3. Ibid.
4. Interview with John Snodgrass, February 2, 2004, hereafter referred to as John Snodgrass interview, Heritage Archives.
5. Letter from Susie Vessels to Bob Burke, April 18, 2004, Heritage Archives.
6. Interview with Richard "Dick" Clements, April 9, 2004, hereafter

referred to as Dick Clements interview, Heritage Archives.
7. Letter from George Lee Stidham to Bob Burke, April 8, 2004, hereafter referred to as Lee Stidham letter, Heritage Archives.
8. Dick Clements interview.
9. Lee Allan Smith interview.
10. Ibid.
11. Interview with Danny Williams, January 28, 2004, hereafter referred to as Danny Williams interview, Heritage Archives.
12. Ibid.
13. Lee Stidham letter.
14. Lee Allan Smith interview and letter from Richard Battles to Lee Allan Smith, undated, Heritage Archives.
15. Interview with Eddie Crowder, January 14, 2004, hereafter referred to as Eddie Crowder interview, Heritage Archives.
16. Ibid.
17. Ibid.
18. Letter from A.F. Williams to Lee Allan Smith, September 10, 1951, Heritage Archives.
19. Undated newspaper article, Heritage Archives.
20. Dee Sadler interview.
21. Ibid.
22. Ibid.
23. Lee Allan Smith interview.
24. Lee Allan Smith interview.
25. Ibid.

four | **to the shores of tripoli**
1. Lee Allan Smith interview.
2. Ibid.

3. Undated article from *Air Force Times,* Heritage Archives.
4. Undated article from *Tripoli Trotter,* the Wheelus Field newspaper, Heritage Archives.
5. Lee Allan Smith interview.
6. Ibid.
7. Ibid.
8. Ibid.
9. Promotional poster, Special Services, Wheelus Field, Heritage Archives.
10. Lee Allan Smith interview.
11. Ibid.
12. Undated article from Wheelus Field base newspaper, Heritage Archives.
13. Ibid.
14. Letter from Colonel Rollen H. Anthis to Commander, 1603rd Air Base Group, November 26, 1954, Heritage Archives.
15. Letter from Colonel B.G. Dilworth to Lee Allan Smith, December 1, 1954, Heritage Archives.

five | **looking for a job**
1. Lee Allan Smith interview.
2. Ibid.
3. David Dary, *The Oklahoma Publishing Company's First Century* (Oklahoma City: Oklahoma Publishing Company, 2003), p. 68-69, hereafter referred to as *The Oklahoma Publishing Company's First Century.*
4. Ibid., p. 70.
5. Ibid., p.
6. Ibid., p. 101.

7. Danny Williams interview.
8. Dick Clements interview.
9. Interview with Jim Greenwald, April 21, 2004, hereafter referred to as Jim Greenwald interview, Heritage Archives.
10. Lee Allan Smith interview.
11. Ibid.
12. Danny Williams interview.
13. Ibid.; www.firststrategy.com/chuckdunaway

six | **deann**
1. Interview with DeAnn Smith, May 3, 2004, hereafter referred to as DeAnn Smith interview, Heritage Archives.
2. Ibid.
3. Ibid.
4. Ibid.
5. Ibid.
6 Ibid.
7. Ibid.
8. Ibid.
9. Ibid.
10. Ibid.
11. Ibid.
12. Ibid.
13. Interview with George Short, May 7, 2004, hereafter referred to as George Short interview.

seven | **broadcasting executive**
1. Executive proclamation of March 15, 1961, Heritage Archives.
2. Letter from Stanley Draper, Jr., to the Judging Committee of the Outstanding Young Man Award, January 15, 1964, Heritage Archives.

3. Ibid.

4. Lee Allan Smith interview.

5. Ibid.

6. Ibid.

7. *The Daily Oklahoman* (Oklahoma City, Oklahoma), April 17, 1966.

8. Lee Allan Smith interview.

9. Interview with Ronnie Kaye, April 2, 2004, hereafter referred to as Ronnie Kaye interview, Heritage Archives.

10. Lee Allan Smith interview.

11. Across the Street menu, Heritage Archives.

12. Ibid.

13. Ed deCordova interview.

14. Lee Allan Smith interview.

15. Letter from William "Bill" Robinson to Bob Burke, January 19, 2005, Heritage Archives.

16. Lee Allan Smith interview.

17. Ibid.

eight | stars and stripes

1. Ibid.

2. *Stars and Stripes Show* program, Heritage Archives.

3. Ibid.

4. Interview with James H. Norick, February 26, 2004, hereafter referred to as James Norick interview, Heritage Archives.

5. *The Daily Oklahoman,* June 30, 1971.

6. Lee Allan Smith interview.

7. Ibid.

8. Stars and Stripes program, Heritage Archives.

9. Lee Allan Smith interview.

10. Ibid.

11. Interview with William C. "Bill" Thrash, January 28, 2004, hereafter referred to as Bill Thrash interview, Heritage Archives.

12. *The Daily Oklahoman,* July 7, 1970.

13. Ibid., July 4, 1971.

14. Ibid.

15. Interview with Ken "Sugar" Smith, April 30, 2004, hereafter referred to as Sugar Smith interview, Heritage Archives.

16. Text of Bob Hope's remarks for 1971 *Stars and Stripes Show*, Heritage Archives.

17. Stars and Stripes program, Heritage Archives.

18. Ibid.

19. Ibid.

20. Ibid.

21 Lee Allan Smith interview.

22. Letter from Bob Hope to Lee Allan Smith, March 18, 1972, Heritage Archives.

23 Ibid.

24. *The Daily Oklahoman,* June 11, 1972.

25. Ibid., June 28, 1972.

26. Stars and Stripes program, Heritage Archives.

27. Ibid.

28. Bill Thrash interview.

29. Ibid.

30. Ibid.

31. *The Daily Oklahoman,* July 8, 1972.

32. Telegram from Billy Graham to Lee Allan Smith, June 29, 1972.

33. George Short interview.

nine | **looking for a job**

1. Interview with DeLee Stephanie Smith, January 15, 2004, hereafter referred to as DeLee Smith interview, Heritage Archives.
2. DeAnn Smith interview.
3. DeLee Smith interview.
4. Ibid.
5. Interview with Jennifer Smith Kiersch, April 19, 2004, hereafter referred to as Jennifer Kiersch interview, Heritage Archives.
6. Ibid.
7. Ibid.
8. Ibid.
9. Interview with Wendy Blythe Smith, hereafter referred to as Wendy Smith interview, April 16, 2004, Heritage Archives.
10. Ibid.
11. Wendy Smith interview.
12. DeLee Smith interview.
13. Ibid.
14. Wendy Smith interview.
15. Ibid.
16. DeAnn Smith interview.
17. George Short interview.
18. Interview with Silkey Wilson, May 10, 2004, Heritage Archives.
19. Ibid.
20. Interview with Ann Smith, January 26, 2004, Heritage Archives.
21. Ibid.
22. Ibid.
23. Letter from Elizabeth Brunsdon to Bob Burke, January 23, 2004, Heritage Archives.
24. Ibid.

ten | **a promoter's promoter**

1. Stars and Stripes program, Heritage Archives.
2. Ibid.
3. Interview with Cathy Kirk, April 21, 2004, hereafter referred to as Cathy Kirk interview, Heritage Archives.
4. Ibid.
5. Ibid.
6. Stars and Stripes program, Heritage Archives.
7. Sugar Smith interview.
8. *The Daily Oklahoman,* July 4, 1975.
9. Ibid.
10. Letter from Jim Greenwald to Lee Allan Smith, July 8, 1975.
11. Stars and stripes program, Heritage Archives.
12. Ibid.
13. *The Daily Oklahoman,* June 20, 1976.
14. Oklahoma City Association of Broadcasters press release, February 10, 1977, Heritage Archives.
15. Letter from Joe Jerkins to Lee Allan Smith, June 19, 1977.
16. Jim Greenwald interview.
17. Interview with Bob Barry, January 14, 2004, hereafter referred to as Bob Barry interview, Heritage Archives.
18. Ibid.
19. Ibid.
20. Ibid.
21. Undated story from *The Daily Oklahoman,* Heritage Archives.

22. Letter from Martha Pat Upp to Bob Burke, April 22, 2004, Heritage Archives.

23. Ibid.

24. Inteview with Joe Washington, February 10, 2004, Heritage Archives.

25. Letter from Bill Banowsky to Bob Burke, April 8, 2004, Heritage Archives.

26. Interview with Fred Zahn, January 29, 2004, Heritage Archives.

27. Letter from James Norick to Bob Burke, April 14, 2004, Heritage Archives.

28. Undated news story from *Journal Record* (Oklahoma City, Oklahoma), Heritage Archives.

29. Interview with Kerry Robertson Kerby, April 2, 2004, Heritage Archives.

eleven | **champion fund raiser**

1. Sugar Smith interview.

2. Interview with Larry Nichols, May 15, 2005, Heritage Archives.

3. Letter from Jackie Cooper to Bob Burke, April 5, 2004, Heritage Archives.

4. Interview with Josie Freede, May 15, 2005, Heritage Archives.

5. George Short interview.

6. *The Daily Oklahoman,* November 25, 1982.

7. Ibid.

8. Letter from Jack T. Conn, November 16, 1982, Heritage Archives.

9. *The Daily Oklahoman,* June 24, 1982.

10. Ibid., April 8, 1985.

11. Undated newspaper stories, Heritage Archives.

12. *The Metro Downtowner* (Oklahoma City, Oklahoma), May 20, 1985.

13. *The Daily Oklahoman,* September 25, 1985.

14. Ibid.

15. Interview with Richard Burpee, January 14, 2004, hereafter referred to as Richard Burpee interview, Heritage Archives.

16. Ibid.

17. Ibid.

18. Lee Allan Smith interview.

19. Bob Barry interview.

20. Ibid.

21. Letter from George Bush to Lee Allan Smith, May 13, 1987, Heritage Archives.

22. Letter from Paul Strasbaugh to Bob Burke, April 14, 2004, Heritage Archives.

23. Ibid.

24. Lee Allan Smith interview.

25. Ray Ackerman interview.

26. Lee Allan Smith interview.

twelve | **oklahoma events**

1. Lee Allan Smith interview.

2. Ibid.

3. Ray Ackerman interview.

4. Interview with Bill Winkler, May 14, 2004, Heritage Archives.

5. Ray Ackerman interview.

6. Undated letter from Jane Jayroe, Heritage Archives.

7. Interview with Sharyn Chesser, January 14, 2004, Heritage Archives.
8. Ibid.
9. Ibid.
10. Ray Ackerman interview.
11. Interview with Clay Bennett, April 6, 2005, hereafter referred to as Clay Bennett interview.
12. Interview with Ed Martin, January 24, 2004, hereafter referred to as Ed Martin interview, Heritage Archives.
13. Ibid.
14. Letter from Jane Jayroe to Bob Burke, February 12, 2004, Heritage Archives.
15. Richard Burpee interview.
16. Ed Martin interview.
17. Ibid.
18. Interview with G.T. Blankenship, April 9, 2004, Heritage Archives.
19. Letter from Burns Hargis to Bob Burke, March 2, 2004, Heritage Archives.
20. Interview with Gene Rainbolt, February 10, 2004, Heritage Archives.
21. Letter from Herman Meinders to Bob Burke February 23, 2004, Heritage Archives.
22. Clay Bennett interview.
23. Letter from Bobby and Kay Murcer to Bob Burke, April 15, 2004, Heritage Archives.
24. Lee Allan Smith interview.
25. Lee Allan Smith interview.
26. *The Journal Record* (Oklahoma City, Oklahoma), November 11, 1992.

27. *The Daily Oklahoman,* December 6, 1992.
28. Interview with Joe Carter, April 1, 2004, Heritage Archives.
29. Lee Allan Smith interview.
30. Letter from Ctaci Combs to Bob Burke, April 20, 2004, Heritage Archives.
31. Jennifer Kiersch interview.
32. Letter from Ctaci Combs to Bob Burke, April 20, 2004, Heritage Archives.
33. Interview with Dave Lopez, September 3, 2004, Heritage Archives, hereafter referred to as Dave Lopez interview.
34. Interview with Kari Watkins, January 29, 2004, Heritage Archives.
35. Dave Lopez interview.
36. Interview with Joe Castiglione, January 16, 2004, Heritage Archives.
37. Ibid.
38. *The Daily Oklahoman,* October 15, 2000.
39. Interview with Pam Newby, March 23, 2004, Heritage Archives.
40. Joe Dan Trigg interview.

thirtenn | **the new century**

1. *The Daily Oklahoman,* May 6, 2001.
2 Ibid.
3. Letter from Jim Couch to Bob Burke, April 15, 2004, Heritage Archives.
4. Ibid.
5. Ibid.

6. Frank Keating letter.

7. Ibid.

8. Burns Hargis letter.

9. Letter from Marion Devore to Bob Burke, April 13, 2004, Heritage Archives.

10. Letter from Robert Naifeh to Bob Burke, April 21, 2004, Heritage Archives.

11. Interview with Sandy Garrett, May 17, 2004, Heritage Archives.

12. Letter from Mike Turpen to Bob Burke, April 27, 2004, Heritage Archives.

13. Letter from Dave Maloney to Bob Burke, April 27, 2004, Heritage Archives.

14. Eddie Crowder interview.

15. Interview with Charles "Chuck" Schroeder, January 28, 2004, Heritage Archives.

16. Letter from Jim Everest to Bob Burke, May 15, 2004, Heritage Archives.

17. Interview with Larry Payton, January 18, 2005, Heritage Archives.

18. Letter from J. Blake Wade to Bob Burke, April 22, 2004, Heritage Archives.

19. Ibid.

20. Ibid.

21. Interview with Edward C. Joullian III, September 1, 2004, Heritage Archives.

22. Letter from Bill Robinson to Bob Burke, January 19, 2005, Heritage Archives.

23. Interview with William E. "Bill" Durrett, September 1, 2004, Heritage Archives.

Index